Grant

The
Life and
Death
of a
Playa

Timmy Ray

authorHOUSE®

AuthorHouse™
1663 Liberty Drive, Suite 200
Bloomington, IN 47403
www.authorhouse.com
Phone: 1-800-839-8640

First published by AuthorHouse 7/20/2009

ISBN: 978-1-4389-2509-7 (sc)

Printed in the United States of America
Bloomington, Indiana

This book is printed on acid-free paper.

The Forward

I, Timothy K. Sawyer, am sitting in this treatment center reflecting on my life. This story is my life—how I was raised in a family that allowed me to see very vividly both sides of life, thus leading me down the path that was destined for destruction. It shows how my life was unmanageable as a child and how I was drawn to trouble even then.

I was a wild child that even at an early age had fleshly desires. I was consumed by perversion and was sexually aware. I watched some of the best players in the world play the games—oh, and how they succeeded, or how I thought they were succeeding. This had me intrigued from the start.

I watched my dad as he went to work and church and played the women. I also watched as all his friends did the same. My dad was more of a player than a pimp. He had a way about him that would make women give him whatever he wanted. He would bring his check to my mom and still had plenty of money.

Along with going to church every Sunday as a child, I spent a lot of time with my older cousins during the week. That's where I learned about pimping, selling drugs, and fast cars. Now I can see how all of this almost cost me my life. Knowing what I know now, I realize it was all part of God's plan to get me where I am today. If I never would've gotten hooked on drugs/alcohol, I never would've been in this treatment center to send you this message.

Parts of the book are very graphic and explicit. I hope it doesn't offend anyone. It's just my story.

I plan to use part of the proceeds from this book to do some good—maybe help some women because of the emotional strain I've caused so many. I want to help others get off drugs. Lord knows, I helped them destroy themselves. If you don't get anything else out of this book, I hope you women pick up some things to not let some slick-ass player like me use you up. For the men, find yourself one woman and take some instruction, and drive your woman wild.

Happy Reading!!

This story takes place back in 1959 in Dayton, Ohio. When Elester and Annie Sawyer got a present, it was a beautiful little baby boy. They named me Timothy, which in biblical terms means "follower of Christ," which in years to come may seem I was anything but that.

I was born in Dayton, Ohio, which was proved to be one of the most gangsta cities in the Midwest. Dayton is a small midwestern city that has always been filled with drugs, prostitution, and a great nightlife. It has always had a very dangerous undertone—meaning, if you got caught in the wrong place at the wrong time, you could come up missing. I learned how to lie, cheat, and steal at an early age. I was born into a family of playas, pimps, and drug dealers. I didn't stand a chance. They didn't all do it full time, but it was enough to teach me some pretty bad habits.

The men in my family were taught how to work at an early age. My family, like most black families, moved north from Alabama and Georgia. They had to work in the fields and go to school. I guess that's where they got their strength from. They were strong as bulls and good looking too. I guess that's partly the reason they could fight so good and get the women too.

In 1962, we moved to St. Louis—that is when the shit kicked in. At an early age, I was already showing some pretty bizarre behavior. I remember hearing through the walls as my mom and dad had sex and being aroused. I didn't know that was what they were doing until I walked in on them one night.

At this time I was getting to be about three or four. I had a babysitter named Mrs. Jones. One day I was talking crazy to Mrs. Jones. I was up running around and making a bunch of noise. I broke a vase. She told me to sit down or she was going to whip me. I replied, "Bitch, you ain't my momma—you can't tell me what to do." That's the first of one of many severe ass whippings. She whipped me, and then when my mom picked me up, she told her what I did and said. When my mom got me home it was on. From there it got worse.

I have an older sister named Esther, who couldn't stand me because people used to call me the pretty baby. I remember it was bedtime and she was lying in the bed watching TV with her knees up in front of her chest. She said something to me that I didn't like. I grabbed a pair of scissors off the nightstand and threw them at her. If it weren't for her knees being in the way, the scissors would have stuck her in the chest. That was ass whipping number three.

Now things were pretty peaceful for a while—parks, amusement parks, and riding the neighbor's boxer—you know, normal kid shit. Then my baby brother Mike was born. My mother asked me what I wanted to name him. I told her Bullwinkle after my favorite cartoon at that time. It wasn't long before I started feeling neglected and started really acting out.

Shortly after, we moved back to Dayton, Ohio. That is when the shit really got freaky. I was five years old by this time and learning really fast. I guess it's because I was so nosy. I was into everything, from throwing rocks at my neighbor's dog to filling my dad's gas tank with water. I thought I was doing him a favor. I didn't know that it wasn't water he was putting in the tank at the gas station. Needless to say, that was another ass whipping. My sister had a friend that used to live down the street. I used to sneak and watch her and my sister fondling each other in the basement. They caught me looking one time; it is a good thing I could run faster than them. They chased me and chased me. If they would have caught me, I'm sure they would have beaten the crap out of me. Her friend never would let me touch that ass. But that still didn't keep me from trying. Then there was a girl that that lived across the street. She was a year or two older than I was. She came over one day and said, "I seen my mom and dad doing something. You want to try it?" Then she started kissing me and pulling my pants down. I didn't know what she was doing, but I liked it and I was trying like hell. This went on all summer. One time, we were in my grandmother's room dry humping and my sister and my cousin were peeping through the keyhole and told my grandmother. I loved my grandmother and she loved me too. I was my grandmother's heart. So she just laughed and told me, "Don't be taking your old women in there in my bed." She knew I wasn't going to bust a grape.

I was always a daredevil. We lived on Germantown Hill. I used to have a little red tractor. I took it up to the top of the hill and rode it down to the bottom. Just as I got there, a car pulled out of the Bonded gas station and I rolled my tractor. It's just by the grace of God that I didn't kill myself. That still didn't stop me from doing it again. I learned how to swim before I could ride a bike. That was cool because I liked to squeeze the girls' asses and pull their swimming trunks down. I don't know why I was so nasty at such an early age.

I probably need to see someone about that. In fact, I'm still pretty nasty; I just control myself a little better today.

I was getting older now—around six or seven years old. My dad became the biggest playa I knew. He took me everywhere with him—including to his girlfriends' houses—and he had women everywhere in town, and out of town. I remember going to Detroit over to some of his girlfriends' houses. He would always have me dance for them. They would get the biggest kick out of it. I was always a good dancer. Then I would go outside and play while he did his thing. After an hour or so, we would leave and go to the next destination. The same thing would happen. They would always offer us something to eat or drink, and I would dance for them and go outside and play. When it was time to go, he would always leave with something, be it money, suits, or both. I thought I was having fun. But I can see now how that probably played a big part in the problems I would have later in life. No child should be forced to keep secrets like that.

When I was in the first grade, my family moved from the city to Jefferson Township. This was the first black suburb in Dayton. I went to Blairwood Elementary and was making new friends. There was just one problem. They probably felt more like sparring partners than friends, because all I wanted to do was fight. It started with the guys on my street, all the way up to three years older than I was. I beat them all. By the time I was eight or nine, boys were coming from two and three streets away to fight me and I would send them home crying. One day, a boy came over with his older sister and a bunch of friends. We were playing at first. We went down to a place where they were building a house. All they had built at the time was the basement. Then he started a fight. I was winning; then they all jumped me and threw me in the basement. There was a man-made ladder that the construction crew had built. That's what I used to get out.

I learned how to fight so well from being around my older cousins. They all were about fifteen to twenty years older than I was. They were always boxing with me and jigging at me. Is that what made me so mean?

By this time, I guess I was getting too old to go with my dad. I guess he didn't want me to know too much. Go figure. By this time, my cousin Jessie took over. He was my favorite. He taught me stuff that no boy my age should ever know. He showed about pimping, selling dope, and fast cars. He would say, "Come on, li'l cuz and ride with me." I would sit in the back of that triple black Fleetwood with my pop and chips and pick up on all the game.

I would go with him to drop off hoes and pick them up. In the middle of all that, he was selling other stuff. To this day, I don't know what he was selling. I do know it was some kind of powder, because there would be some left on his nose and in his mustache. Every now and then, he would get a little rough with his girls for being short with his money or getting too high.

We would go over to my other cousin's house sometimes and I would watch them build racecars. I guess that is where I get my love for speed. Jessie, Robert, and Amos (Rabbit) had fast cars. They used to race in front of West Town Shopping Center on West Third Street. That was so much fun, riding with them. They would pool their money, so no matter which one of them won, they all would win.

During all this time, my family would go to church every Sunday all day. We would go to morning service, and since my mom and dad both had quartet groups, we were always at one service or another. That's where I got my love for the Lord and my love for music, although the message got very confused, because I saw all kinds of church people doing all kinds of things—from drinking to going with other people's wives or husbands. It was always funny when someone got caught. It's funny because the quartet field had groupies just like R & B. That's why for the longest time I thought it was OK to be married and have other women.

In fact, there were a couple of tragedies as a result of all this messing around. One of the guys in the group was married and killed his girlfriend because she was going to leave him. One of the other guy's wife killed him. She claimed he had jumped on her. But no one will ever know. And she didn't do a day in jail.

By the time I was twelve, I was playing bass guitar. I started out playing lead guitar. Then I switched to bass. I got real good real fast. I started out playing in a band with some people from my school. We would play songs from groups like the Ohio Players; Earth, Wind and Fire; The Bar-Kays; and so on. These were some fun times. We played in a couple of talent shows. I started getting recognition from the girls now.

My dad had a group called the Evangelist Singers. Johnny, his guitar player, told him that if I could play songs off the radio, I could probably play for them. I guess my dad wasn't ready for that yet. It was a few years before I started playing with them. But when I did, it was really cool being able to travel with my dad again. Also, being around all the other guys in the group helped me to grow up real fast. It was kind of like having eight fathers instead of one, because I learned from all of them.

I always had the finer things in life, from tailor-made suits to the freshest bikes. That is right—twelve years old and wearing tailor-made suits. My mom and dad made great money, plus whatever my dad hustled from his women. Things were good. He also had dump trucks—three of them. I used to ride with him sometimes. He was truly my hero. He would work all night and mess with his hoes. Then he'd come home and get some sleep and get up and work his trucks, and he did this every day. Sometimes the trucks would break and I would help him work on them. I was helping him do everything from changing transmissions to changingring-and-pinion gears . That is where my mechanical ability came from.

My uncle Sonny was another one of my heroes. He was my mother's brother. He would come over to the house and visit every week. At this time, my mother had a nephew that lived across the street and a niece that lived next door. My uncle and her husband and my cousin across the street used to drink together. My uncle used to hide his bottles behind my mother's couch, and I was slipping in them every chance I got. I knew what it was because when I was younger, my uncle was letting me have little sips every now and then. At this time a lot of things were going on in my life. I was enjoying the taste of alcohol by now, because since I was ten my uncles were slipping drinks in me behind my mother's back. I was thirteen, and I was into everything—drinking, smoking weed, and playing in the band, and, oh yes, the girls. If it could be done I was doing it. I used to hang out with guys a lot older than I was that lived down the street. These were some of the most gangster cats I knew. Street gangs, cars, drugs, liquor, weed, girls, and wine were all going down. One day, a couple of them and I went across the creek to this man's property and we stole cherries out of his cherry tree. When he came out of the house, he blasted us with rock salt. Man, that creek water never felt so good.

One of them was teaching me how to drive. As long as I had some gas money or a joint, we were riding. He had a '68 Pontiac Tempest. We would drive all over the back roads of Jefferson Township. It was kind of scary at first. The roads were kind of narrow and hilly. When cars would be coming towards us, sometimes I would weave off the road. He would grab the wheel and get us back on the road. But I got the hang of it in no time.

By this time, my uncle Sonny had taken the place of my dad pretty much. I would stay over at his house a lot; he would even let me bring Sparky, my German shepherd. She would stay in his basement, until one day she tried to bite him. That ended that. Uncle Sonny used to give me anything I wanted. He used to give me money just about anytime I asked. I got tired of just asking him for money, mainly because I felt like he was getting tired of giving it to me. So I devised a plan. I started washing his cars and cutting his grass. That was enough to keep me in wine and weed.

At the age of fifteen, I started playing in my dad's group (the Evangelist Singers). Isn't that the way—sin all week and then try to cover it up with praising God on Sunday. I am so glad he is a forgiving God, because the years to come would prove I surely did need it. I was slowly becoming just like my dad and his cronies. The first rule I lived by and still live by today, my dad told me as soon as he thought we should have the birds and bees talk. He gave some advice that went like this: if all a woman has to give you is some sex, you do not need her, because you can get sex anywhere. That is why I always went for older girls. Most times I stuck to that, but sometimes I just had to have some sex. If they wanted me to hang around, the money came later. He also used to tell me that you're not wrong until you get caught—more words of wisdom.

While I was playing in my dad's group, we were going everywhere. All the guys in the group worked, and I was still in school. So we went anywhere we could get to within twelve hours. So when we left to come back, they could go to work and I could get to school. I had been halfway over the country by the time I got out of high school. While playing with them, I recorded a few records, and was on stage and TV more times than I can remember.

One weekend we went to Davenport, Iowa. We had concerts Saturday night and Sunday afternoon. There were a few groups ahead of us; we were the headliners. While we were sitting waiting to go on, this sweet young lady caught my attention. She had no idea who I was. I said, "Hello, how are you today?"

"Fine," she replied.

I said, "You sure are." Then she gave this little schoolgirl smile. So we made a little small talk—you know, the usual. What's your name, where are you from, do you have a boyfriend? I told her I was with the Evangelist Singers.

She said, "Really? I heard that your group was really good."

I said, "We're alright." I found out she was older than I was; this made her even more attractive.

So it came time for us to go onstage. We hit the floor; we were dead sharp too, as always. Man, we were really putting it down. I was playing a Fender precision fretless bass guitar. This used to amaze a lot of the other groups. They would stand in the back and watch me work. They would say, "How does he play like that without frets?" Down about the middle of the show I recognized a woman sitting in front. She gaped her legs wide open. All I could see was bush. I guess James saw it too, because he forgot a couple words to the song. But we turned it out as usual.

After we came offstage, she was waiting outside for me. She said, "That was great." She said, "I heard all those guys from the other group back there talking about you." She said she had no idea what they were talking about, but they seemed pretty impressed. So she waited while we loaded the equipment onto the van. When we were finished she gave me her number and a kiss. She said, "I hope I get to see you again."

I said, "I'll have to see what we can do about that." So it turns out that my dad and a couple other guys in the group had met someone also. On the way home, they were scheming on a way to get back up there the next weekend. I said, "I want to go."

My dad laughed and said, "I figured you did." So about Monday or Tuesday I called the old girl and told her that we were coming back up there the next weekend. You could have heard her screaming for miles, she was so excited.

So the weekend came and we were on our way. My dad told my mom they still owed us some money and we were going to get it. So we got there and checked in the hotel. I called my friend and she came right over. It was a nice, warm Iowa spring night. It had rained earlier, so there were puddles still on the ground. So after I got changed, we walked and got something to eat. On our way back to the hotel, we had to walk under an overpass. There was a big puddle of water in the street. A car came speeding through the overpass and splashed water all over us. We were so mad at first. Then we looked at each other and laughed and held each other and kissed. We were soaked. So we get back to the room and take off our wet clothes. Man, what timing. That time I didn't have to persuade anyone to take off their clothes. You know what came next. Those old guys talked about me all the way home. They thought that was my first piece.

I grew up real fast. It seems like I went from a boy to a man overnight. Over the next few years, I would learn so much it was crazy. I learned respect for myself and other people. I had respect for women as long as I could get in their panties and get some money. And that's when I started to learn how to play women. I mean, girls were coming from everywhere just because I was in the group and could play the bass real good and was fairly handsome. I was six-teen now and learning how to sling dick pretty good. I had girls in Davenport, Iowa; Harrisburg, Pennsylvania; and Detroit. It seems like everywhere we went, there was always some girl that wanted to talk to me. I watched a whole lot of young ladies grow up and I was trying to help all I could.

I used to go to Harrisburg, Pennsylvania, and stay for the sum-mer—boy, was that fun. My cousins and I used to go to Kline Vil-lage and carry people's groceries to their cars. Sometimes we would do pretty good; sometimes we wouldn't. Once, my cousin and I and a friend of ours made about ten dollars apiece. We decided we wanted to get some wine. We weren't old enough, so we had to get someone to buy it for us. We walked down on Market Street to the liquor store and gave some money to a wino to buy it for us. When he came out, he didn't want to give us our wine. As we were walking up Market Street, my cousin was on one side of the wino and our friend was on the other. I was walking behind them. They were arguing with him, trying to get him to give us our wine. He said, "I ain't giving you punks shit." So as we approached the corner, I ran around and snatched one bag and Dave grabbed the other one and we ran across Market Street. We didn't stop until we were about a block away. We turned around to look back; the wino was on the corner jumping up and down screaming at us. Man, was he pissed. He brought it on himself, though. He should have just given us what we paid for and we wouldn't have taken both his bottles. Man, we got drunk that night.

Now, when I turned sixteen, I got my license. I had a job and looked old enough to go to the liquor store; a lot of times my uncle Sonny would send me in. Uncle Sonny and I were real close. I think this made some of my other family members jealous. They never wanted to do anything to help him. So whenever there was some work to be done, I was always there. Uncle Sonny had a little yellow cup that he kept in the car. We would pour shots of gin and ride around drinking. I came to realize why he would always drive so slow. I'll bet we never reached forty miles per hour once.

John Boyd, who is deceased now, was one of my best friends. He and I used to get together and play our guitars, drink wine, and smoke weed. This was my first real experience I had in how friends would turn on you when they got jealous of you. I guess it was just a little too much—me going to see some girl and coming over to his house and letting him smell my fingers. He always thought I was so fortunate because I had it all, so he thought. I guess now that I look back on it, what more could a teenager want? I had a job, my own car, girlfriends, I could get into adult clubs, and had the all the weed I needed. I guess I did have it lightweight going on. John hating onme is one of the things that made me grow up. It really hurt me that a friend that I had grown up with could turn on me like that. That takes me to another lesson my dad taught me: if you are going to do wrong, do it by yourself, so that is what I did.

I was in my sophomore year in high school. My heart was all wrapped up in Alicia—in fact, I still wonder today where she is and how she is doing. She was the most beautiful girl in the world to me. In a way, I'm glad she got away, because I would have probably screwed up her life too. I think I was a little too gangsta for her parents. There was a guy named Leon that liked her. How he got my parents' number I don't know. But he called me and told me not to call her anymore. So the next day I drove my mom's car up to their school looking for him. As I was walking through the school, I happened to come across their class. Alicia seemed so happy to see me. Dude just happened to be sitting beside her. He looked as nervous as a whore in church. He knew why I was there, so he told the teacher, and the teacher told the principal. Dude got some of his buddies to walk him to the bus so I wouldn't whip that ass. Needless to say, her principal called her mom; her mom called mine. Shortly after that they moved.

That summer I turned seventeen, I was going into my junior year in high school. All the skills were in full tilt now. I was going to take auto mechanics at the Joint Vocational School. There were so many people signed up they added another class; they called it extended day, which was cool by me. That meant I didn't have to be there until noon, which gave me plenty of time to get some weed, roll a few joints, drink a beer, and get to school in time for lunch and get paid. Everything I had been taught up until that point kicked in. All of a sudden I was the man. I was ready to take the helm.

I was seventeen and acted older than most guys nineteen or twenty. I finally was getting just about everything I wanted. I had a job, and my game was kicking in also. The only thing missing was the pimping, and I would have been just like big cuz. I was having so much fun traveling, playing music, working, and selling weed life was good. I and some friends of mine formed a band. We started playing a few gigs, then the girls started coming. You know how they like singers and musicians. Now the girls started stacking up. I started the other level of the game. I had a lot of girls that liked me but I was only looking for certain ones. If they didn't have their own cars, jobs, and cribs, I didn't want to be bothered. So naturally, it was older women. That's where I started learning how to please women. My dad, my cousin, and some of my dad's friends would tell me stuff. But it was nothing like hands-on training.

My sister was going to Wright State University. One weekend she asked me if I wanted to come up for the weekend. I said sure. It ends up I was supposed to stay in the guys' dorm with a friend of hers. She left and went up to Oxford. I ended up staying in the room with her roommate smoking weed and drinking. There were drunk, naked girls everywhere. Needless to say, I had a field day.

By my senior year I had it down. I knew the right things to say to get into the girls' minds, their draws, then in their purses. I had one special girl. I didn't think of her like that. She wasn't a hoe. In fact, she was a virgin when I hit it, or so she said. That was some good shit too. She kind of had me sprung. We spent so much time together I started letting my other business slip. It started out just kissing and grinding on each other. Then one day she let me hit it. After that we were doing it every chance we got. Then she got pregnant and the kind of parents she had would have made us get married. So I talked her into getting an abortion.

Shortly after high school I moved to North Carolina. The Carolina girls really liked the brother. It was so easy because it was nothing but wide open space, and a bunch of little cities in between. I was dropping off one and picking up another. I had become my dad. Clothes and money were rolling in now. My dope game was strong too. I don't know if I was fearless or just stupid. I never gave any thought to whose business I was taking or whose girlfriend I was screwing.

My cousin Vette was selling dope also. So needless to say, we clicked like a mutha. We would go to Charlotte and bring weed and coke back and just tear those other cats' asses out of the frame. With him being country sly and I being city slick, we had it going on. It was funny how we could be so far apart and be so much alike.

These were some of the best times in my life. I was eighteen and wild—I mean, I really didn't give a damn. I was the new kid on the block. The guys looked up to me, and the girls loved me. I guess I was a novelty—the first one to move in from up the road, as they say. My cousin and I stayed in Charlotte all the time—parties at Freedom Park, and going over to different girls' cribs and going to club after club. I liked the little country clubs, and the bootleg joints were everywhere. We would drink shots of vodka, gin, and Canadian Mist and chase them with beer. That's also when I tried my first shot of moonshine. I was getting drunk every day, and having sex every night when I wasn't gambling or too drunk.

I came back to Dayton for about a year. My girl and I still had feelings for each other. So we kind of picked up where we left off. I enrolled in Sinclair Community College for the winter quarter, and it really got to be fun because there were all kinds of women there. It turned out to be business as usual.

The school had an activity area next to the cafeteria where everybody hung out. I would sell a lot of weed there. I also got pretty good at shooting pool, and talking shit. And the bad part about it is that I could back it up.

I met women from all over the city, and surrounding areas also. Like this girl from Franklin—this was one of the sweetest girls I had ever met, but she just didn't have her own place, car, and no money either. So you know what they say—three strikes, you're out.

By the summer of 1979 it was back to the Carolinas. This time I moved on the other side of Kings Mountain. It wasn't a very big city, but it had a lot of area and a bunch of shit to get into. Plus it was even closer to Charlotte, right between Shelby and Gastonia. And it was only about two and a half hours from Atlanta. Straight down 85. This proved to be the best geographical spot to be in.

Things really picked up. I got a crew of cats that I ran with now. A couple of them were hustling with me; the others were there to keep me from getting my hands dirty. I don't know why they felt they had to protect me. I guess because I was the baby of the crew. But I was also the most vicious. I was still pretty good with my hands and feet. Plus I kept some heat somewhere around at all times. Come to find out it was good that my boys were with me because there were some jealous cats plotting on me.

It was Mike my right-hand man, Wayne, Paul, and Pig, and I. We were thick as thieves; we had Robertsdale sewed up. We had the women, the drugs, and the liquor. We just went in and set up shop. That is what the other cats couldn't stand. Plus they remembered me from running with Vette. I had to smack a couple of them up. So I already had a rep and was known for packing heat.

I guess you could say that Dolly was my main chick. I had to get her straight, though. When I first got with her she burnt me. But the pussy was so good I couldn't let her go. Plus she treated a brother real swell. A brother had whatever he wanted. Then things just got better and better.

My cousin hooked me up with one of her friends named Minny. That was pay dirt. She had a good ass job she was fine and she was generous. That was my first rolling blow job. We were on our way from Shelby to Kings Mountain. She asked me if I could hold it in the road. I said, "What?" Then she started zipping down my pants, and I said, "Oh!!" I found out that it took a little more driving skills than I had at the time to get a blow job while I was driving. She was pretty kinky. She tried forever to get me to eat her pussy. But that was something I just couldn't do. One day we were lying in the bed. She took her hand and wiped it on her pussy and put it on my mouth. That almost got her ass kicked. But I made her get up and get out of my house. When she left, I noticed that it didn't smell bad. I licked my lips and it didn't taste bad either. I said, "Hmmmm, could this be another tool." If she wanted me to do it so bad, the girls must really like it. I couldn't wait to try it out. And as you will soon see, I got pretty good at it also.

Then there was Myrna; she was about five foot eight, 140 pounds, sexy lips, and the biggest pretty brown eyes you would ever want to see. I met her when I was out putting in applications. She was a security guard at a tool company. She lived in Gastonia. I know what you are thinking—a job, yes a job. Through all my hustling I always had a job. I just loved money no matter where it came from.

Being with Myrna was different. She had three beautiful children. So when I hooked up with her, I went straight into parenthood. It was all good because she had enough family in the area to watch them whenever we wanted to go out. The sex was wild and crazy. When I made love to her, it would look like I had been in a tiger pit. My back would be all ate up. When I ate her noo noo—yes, for some reason, I couldn't wait to eat her pussy. After I tasted what Minny had left on my lips, it didn't seem so bad after all. And I was right—it was another tool, probably the best one of all. And it worked out pretty good, because she liked to have it done and I became addicted to the way that long, slender chocolate body would flex and pulsate when I did it. I think that was more of a turn-on than screwing. I thought she was truly in love; there was not anything she wouldn't do for me. I kept her car, I ate real good, and her money was my money.

Things were really off the hook now all my cats thought I was the king. Myrna and Minny both drove a 1974 Grand Prix. One was triple white and the other one was blue and white. With Minny in Shelby and Myrna in Gastonia, I could switch up whenever I wanted to. The brother had it going on. Then one day it came to an end with Myrna and me.

Myrna's ex-husband came to town. They were supposed to be going to sign papers so the kids could get his military benefits, and they stayed out all night. It was plain to see they had been fucking. He had put passion marks all over her neck. When I saw that, I jumped straight up in the bed. I went to the closet and she ran out the door; she thought I was getting ready to shoot her. That's where I kept my sawed-off shotgun. Instead, I packed my clothes and moved back to Kings Mountain.

Things were never the same with me after that. I guess I was hurt more than I knew. It took me awhile to get over that. So I said that I would never let my feelings get involved again. The playa was crushed. For a while I still had Dolly and Minny. Then I just went crazy. I just didn't care anymore. I was twenty now, and these hoes couldn't tell me shit. I got real gutter with it. I started being seen with the other girls by the other girls and didn't give a shit. I felt like it would turn out like me and Myrna anyway, so what the fuck.

Then I started messing around with Dolly's cousin Dora for a little while just to stir up some shit. That didn't last long, because she was just cute. I mean really fine. She was a cheerleader at Wingate College. She was about five foot seven, 130 pounds., and black as coal. I mean sexier than a mutha. She had some of the fattest pussy lips and when they got wet they shined like new money. Inside was the prettiest shade of pink, soft as a rose petal and a scent as fresh as spring rain.

After her was Vivian, another star. She was probably the sweetest on the surface, but she was a red girl. I could tell that she had a temper, and those country girls didn't mind cutting a brother. I always said a good run was better then a bad stand any day and it was time. By this time, I was twenty-one and the coldest in the Carolinas at my game. One day I had told Dora I would take her back to school. While we were in the bedroom Vivian pulled up. When she came in, I told her that I was taking a friend back to school and I would get with her later. When I went back in the room, Dora told me she had heard everything I said. I said, "Are you ready to go?" At this time in my life I didn't give a damn about what women thought about what I said or did.

It was 1981. I had graduated from local shit to taking my game on the road. I would take weed to Ohio and bring powder back to Carolina, and always had a bad broad with me. Then I had met Gina #1. She was five foot eight, 145 pounds, high yellow, long pretty hair, hazel eyes, big old ass, titties, and thighs. Just thick for no damn reason she would cook, clean, and go to work, and of course she was very generous. Gina was so sweet. And when it came to sex, she could go all night. And I would be hanging right there with her. She didn't care where we did it either. Man, she turned me on.

Now Gina also had a brother named Milton; he was cool as hell. We hit a couple licks together. One time we were in Charlotte messing around, and we pulled on to J.C. Smith campus. We were sitting there smoking some weed, while a few cars down a female campus police officer was looking dead at us. While I was watching her walk toward us, I was telling Milton to put the joint out. He said, "Huh?"

I said, "Put the damn joint out." By that time she was at the car.

When she tapped on the window, Milton said, "Oh, shit." So when I rolled the window down, the biggest cloud of smoke you have ever seen rolled out at the officer.

She stepped back and said, "What the hell do y'all think you're doing?" I started begging instantly, because I didn't want her to call the police. Shit, I must have had about five grand on me and a couple of pounds of weed.

I said, "Please, ma'am, please let us go and we will never come back here again." I guess I must have been looking real pitiful, because she was laughing her ass off and then told us to leave, and not let her see us on campus again. So we got the hell out of there as fast as we could.

In the summer of 1982, I got a call from my sister. She was in air traffic controller school in Oklahoma City, Oklahoma. She asked me if I wanted to move out there. So I said sure. It was about time for me to get out of Kings Mountain anyway. I had heard that I was being watched, so this was as good a time as any before I got busted. I didn't want to go to prison anywhere, let alone North Carolina. It was tough for a black man on the streets; I knew I didn't want to give them that kind of control over me.

So I asked my cat Barry if he wanted to go with me and he said he would. We started getting my car together; we did the brakes and changed the oil. When we did the test drive, my brake line busted. My car had been sitting so long the brake line rusted. I was driving so many other cars I didn't drive mine much.

After a week or so, we took off. It turned out to be an excursion. We got down to Gaffney and started across Highway 11. My power steering pump was too full and it started spitting out fluid, and my motor mount caught on fire. So we took some ice and water out of the cooler and poured it on the motor mount and put the fire out. Then off we went again. I took off driving, because I didn't trust anybody driving in the mountains at night but me. I got us through the mountains and let Barry drive. I went to sleep and we had gotten almost to Nashville. I woke up and we were almost out of gas. Barry had never done much traveling, so he didn't know to start looking for gas early. This was in 1982, so there weren't as many gas stations that stayed open all night as there are now. So we pulled over and slept in the gas station parking lot until they opened.

We took off from there. It seemed like it took us forever to get out of Tennessee, and Arkansas was even worse. We got almost to Little Rock and the front seal went out in my transmission. Barry and I walked about a mile to an auto parts store and bought some transmission stop-leak and put it in the transmission. We took off from there and it never leaked again.

We hit Oklahoma City and things just felt right. We went out to the FAA training center where my sister was to get her key. When I got to her class, I was already scoping it out for women, but there were none to be found. On the way to the apartment the scenery quickly changed. It was a nice middle-class suburban area. Shopping centers, strip malls, and restaurants were everywhere; so were the girls. I mean all kinds—Mexican, Oriental, Native Americans, white, and of course my sweet Nubian queens. I mean it was on tilt. I had never seen this much variety before. I was as happy as a sissy with a bag of dicks. So we got to the apartment and got the trailer unloaded, put everything in order, and waited for my sister to get home.

When she made it in, we sat around and talked for a bit. Then it was off to see the sights. That didn't last long, because I guess we were tired from the trip. The first thing on the agenda was to get some money. Since we were in a strange place, this meant getting a job. Barry got a job pretty quick; it took me a minute. I guess I wasn't real serious about working. I didn't want to just take any old thing. Besides, it was fun lying around the pool messing with the girls. There were a bunch of them in the complex.

Money was getting low and I was getting a little more desperate. So I got a job at McDonald's as a maintenance man. It was the highest-paying job there next to the store manager. Barry left to go back to North Carolina after losing his money in Lincoln Park in a three-card molly game. I saw it coming a mile away. A guy and a girl were walking through the park arguing like he had beaten her out of some money. They asked us if we wanted to try the game, while the girl edged us on. So I said, "What the hell." I lost ten dollars and quit. Barry lost all his money. I tried to get him to stop, but he insisted he put up his jewelry to get his money back. And you know what happened then. That's right—not only did he lose his money, but his jewelry was gone now too. This upset Barry so bad, he called his girl as soon as we got to the house and told her to send him some money so he could come home. There was a motorcycle on the other side of the apartments. I told him to take the tags off of it late one night and put them on his bike and ride it home. I told him by the time they missed them, he would be in Carolina. He was too scared to do it. So she sent the money and he left.

With Barry being gone, that left me just like I like it, flying solo. It was almost like I had been there all my life. I had met some pretty good connects as far as getting drugs. Barry and I had met a guy in the park one day; his name was V.J. He hooked us up with some weed, and it was on from then on. V.J. had a girl he was kicking it with. We used to go hang out with her and her sisters. Something just didn't feel right though. Come to find out they were getting high on more than weed. They were smoking angel dust and this other thing they called a super cool. They would take a cigarette and dip it in embalming fluid, let it dry out, and then smoke it. I tried it once. It didn't do anything for me, so I never did it again. One day we were riding around drinking E&J and smoking weed laced with angel dust. When we stopped the car and got out, I stumbled around in circles for it seemed about five minutes trying to get my balance. I really didn't like that, so needless to say, I never tried that again. Slowly I got away from them. I didn't like the other drugs they were doing. And V.J.'s girlfriend's sisters just weren't doing anything for me. They were cute and had nice bodies but that's about it—no jobs, no money, and houses full of kids. Every dime they got, they were trying to get high, so how could they help me?

My sister finally finished her training and got a job back home. I had met some friends in the complex, so I stayed with them for a while. The one guy I met was a lot younger than I was, but he was a cool young dude. I had met his mom and she said I could stay with them until I got on my feet. I believe she had other intentions. It was his mom's apartment. He had a fine-ass sister too. My dumb ass blew it that time. Instead of chasing her, I should have been after his mother. But she was too far out the realm as far as looks went.

Even though I had gotten a job at McDonald's as a maintenance man, and was one of the highest-paid employees there, this still wasn't good enough—you know how greedy I was. I always had to have more.

Soon I got the break that I was looking for. I was trying to get a job where I made more money. I picked up a paper and it had an ad in it for a sales position, so I said, "What the hell." I put in an application and got the job. I worked both jobs for a while—at least until I got my first check for thirteen hundred dollars for one week. I said to myself, *You mean you can make this kind of money just talking to people?* I quit McDonald's. I said, "If this is all I have to do is talk to people to make this kind of money, I'm in." This was better than selling dope. It was great. I was twenty-two years old in a fifty-thousand-dollar-a-year income bracket. In 1982 that was a lot of money.

I started hanging out with a few of the people I worked with. There were nights of clubbing, wild parties, and women. This was also the beginning of the end, although I did not know it at the time.

There was a brother at work I used to run with named Don—a slim, brown-skinned brother with a perm. We hit a few licks and he showed me around Oklahoma City. He got me hooked up with the side of the city I was trying to get to. He had turned me on to a few hoes, but they were more about getting high than getting money. He claimed to be a pimp, but that was questionable because if he was, why was he still living with his mother? I guess he was really just pimping her. Then the worst thing that could have happened, happened. He showed me how to cook and smoke cocaine. I instantly liked it—too much, I might add. I found myself spending more money than I should. Then I realized that he wasn't shit. Since I was making all the money, he was using me to get high.

So I broke away for a while and I met the finest woman I had ever met I at the time. Sandra was about five foot eleven, 145 pounds, light brown skin, slightly bowlegged, big brown eyes, and a super-size fro. Damn, she was fine. She reminded me of a light-skinned Cleopatra Jones. She lived in Midwest City across from Tinker Air Force Base. I thought we were getting pretty close. I don't know what happened—all of a sudden I couldn't get in touch with her. Maybe it was good, because I was sprung on cocaine. I probably would have ended up messing up her life like I did mine.

Then I met another girl from the east side. She was sexy too, a big-butt freak with a house and a decent job. I think she worked for Lockheed or something like that. I moved in with her, then I found out she liked to get high also. That turned into some serious freak sessions. We did it on my motorcycle. We even did it in the club.

One night she picked out a table in the corner in the dark. I often wore jeans with no underwear. I know it sounds kind of nasty, but that was the times—free spirit and free love. Not to mention that by this time I was a freak as well. We sat at the table. It was real dark. She had on a sundress with no panties, so as we sat there, I put my arms around her and pulled the front of her dress up. As we kissed, I was rubbing on her vagina and she was rubbing my penis through my jeans. She got wetter and wetter and I got harder and harder. I was a bit apprehensive, this was something new for me, so I was really turned on. As she started to pant from the excitement, she unzipped my pants and pulled it out and sat on my lap. She was so wet, it felt like someone turned on a sprinkler. I think this lasted for ten or fifteen minutes. She was so calm it seemed like she had done this before. I didn't care. It started getting good for both of us, and it's good the music was loud, because she let out a couple of loud sighs. I had to keep her from moving so much so everyone wouldn't know what we were doing. It was hard for me to control myself also. She was slowly gyrating around and around, and slowly moving up and down. I could feel her vagina gripping and popping. Then it happened. Bam!!! It was an explosion like we never had before. I mean, it was cum everywhere. When we left, I had to walk close behind her so that no one could see how wet my pants were. That is probably the wildest sexual thing I have ever done to this day. I could hardly ride my bike home I was so weak. Needless to say, we both fell into a deep sleep.

After that, she introduced me to some of her friends. They also got high. So then I started supplying them. It seemed like everything was going well. Little did I know the turn of events that was about to happen.

My car broke down on me shortly after I got my first paycheck. But I had my motorcycle and I was always riding with Don or someone; plus Rise had a car, so I wasn't really worried about it then. It turned out that the sweet job I had was drying up. It had been a week or so since I made a sale, so they let me go. That meant I had to rely on my game, which I had not had time to build up yet. I never got my car fixed as a result. In fact, they had it towed from the apartment complex where I lived. I had to make a decision—turn and run or try and make a go of it. I never had too much rabbit in my blood, so I went for one last stand.

By this time, the girl I was staying with was on my back to give her money. She had gotten laid off. Then I remembered what had happened with Myrna and I had said I wasn't going to give another woman shit. So one morning I was on my way out and we got into a heated discussion about money. She said to me, "You are laying up here fucking me all night, eating my food, and I keep your hair done. You should give me something."

So I said, "Me helping with the utilities, and rent, don't mean shit, ha? What do you want me to do—leave some money on your pillow every morning when I leave? If it's like that, you need to get off your ass and get out there and sell some of that pussy you've been giving me."

Then came the waterworks. She said she thought we had more than that between us.

I said, "What—just because you fuck me and feed me?" I explained to her what had happened before.

Then she said, "Tim, I love you." I told her she should have let me know how she really felt about me. I held her and kissed her forehead. It shocked her. She said, "Damn, how did you flip that shit like that?" Then she ripped my clothes off and we made love again.

Now money was getting low and so was the product, so I came up with a brilliant idea to pawn my motorcycle. Since I did not have the title, he only gave me six hundred dollars. I put that with what I had and bought an ounce. That stuff was pretty good, so I could take a little out for us and still make about a one-thousand-dollar profit.

One of her friends, named Thomas, said he would help me sell it. She said it was cool, so I gave him the majority of it so I wouldn't mess it up. The next couple of days I went to pick up some money and get some for me and Don to cook. He gave me two hundred dollars and a gram. When we got back to the house to cook it, it was nothing but cut. We immediately went back. Thomas was nowhere to be found. So we went and bought me a nine and some gin. We rode the hood looking for him. I knew I would never get the rest of my goods or my money, so I was just going to kill him and be done with it. We finally ran up on him and his brother at the spot. His brother had seen me when I bailed out to the car with the gun in my hand and skirted off. I fired off about six rounds and took out some windows and a tire. I don't know if I hit one of them or not, and I didn't have time to check because porch lights started coming on, so Don and I left. I went back to the house and called my mother and told her I was coming home. This was good timing, because I called the bus station and there was a bus leaving in an hour. So within an hour and a half I was on a bus back to Dayton, and that was the end of the Oklahoma City experience.

I had talked to Don a few days later. He told me that I didn't get him. I had always said when I got some money I was going to go back and finish the job. Things got so good back home I just forgot about it.

It was the Christmas of 1982. My brothers were home from the service. They picked me up at the bus station. It was good seeing them. I had not seen them in about two years, and I guess we all kind of changed. I picked up weight, had my hair down to my shoulders, and was all suited up, even fresh off the bus—a little musty but still sharp. My brothers were looking good also. They had thickened up a little bit. They were fresh out of boot camp, with military haircuts— not the same little boys I left in North Carolina.

So we went to Mom's and put my clothes up. We kicked it with Mom for a little while. I took a shower and changed clothes. Then it was off to the liquor store; we rode around, drank, and talked. As we were riding down Third Street, Mike said, "Do y'all want to pick up a hooker?" These boys were so silly I didn't know if they were playing or not.

So we pulled up on this one and the window went down. I said, I guess they weren't playing. She was on my side, so I asked her how much for the three of us. She said seventy-five dollars. I talked her down to fifty dollars, and made sure she had some rubbers. I had never done this before; I guess GIs were used to it. So she got in the car and we went to her spot. We made a little small talk; we told her that we were brothers and she said she had never done brothers before. So we had a couple of drinks, and I said I was going first. So we took our clothes off. It was hard for me to be excited. I wasn't used to picking up hookers.

She said, "You are not even hard."

I said, "You know what to do to get it hard, don't you?"

She said, "You must be the oldest." So she started sucking it. I really didn't want to fuck her anyway. So I came in her mouth. Then I put my clothes on and waited for Mike and Darryl to get finished. Then we left there and hit a couple of clubs.

The next day, I cleaned up the Caddy and went to pick up my partner, Gary. Now Gary and I were partners since high school. We were the regulators in the ninth grade. Our principal relied on us to help keep trouble down and we were causing most of it. One time, Gary, Vernon, and I were working on the bulletin board in front of the office. One of the teachers came by and said that it was very colorful. Then Vernon said, "It kind of stands out—like your blouse." She just laughed and walked off. We had a bet on who would hit it first. But the art teacher had that sewed up.

Gary and I went and did a little Christmas shopping and drinking at the mall. We were also smoking some killer weed. Gary had some good-ass weed. He had a white dude in Miamisburg he dealt with. So we kicked it for a little while. He told me that a new club called Spunky's was opening up on Christmas. It was right up the street from my mother's. Come to find out my fifth-grade teacher was opening it up. That did not surprise me a bit, because he was probably one of the coolest cats I knew.

Christmas Day came and the whole family was at my mom's. We had to wait on Aunt Liz to come so we could open the gifts. She came and we opened the gifts and ate breakfast. Those were some good times back then. Sometimes I wish we could get those days back, but life goes on. Later on that evening, I got dressed and went and picked up Gary. Little did I know how big a mark we were about to make.

Gary put me down with some weed; he also had some pills and liquor. We fell off into Spunky's and ran into all the old high school cats. It was like a class reunion. They did not know who I was at first, because I had not seen them since graduation. When I left, I was wearing glasses and an afro. Now it was contacts, double-breasted suits, flats, and a curl down to my shoulders. Some of the cats started calling me Morris.

They had some broads out of Fairborn. Not only were they checking us out, but there were girls all over the club saying, "Who are those niggas?" We were sitting at our table and one walks up and introduces herself. She sat and talked for a minute; then her sister and their friend came off the dance floor and joined us. I bought some drinks and we danced and had a ball. I could see T-Bone and they were getting a little heated. The girls had completely forgotten about them. It was getting about time for the club to close, so I asked them if they wanted to go with us. T-Bone really got pissed then. So we left the club and went to my mom's and partied until about four or five in the morning. Mike and Darryl came in about 3:00 a.m.; they said, "What the hell are y'all doing?" It was Gary, me, and three fine hoes. This started the reign of the Tim and Gary show.

So things went on from there. Gary and I would go from club to club selling weed and pills. We would always end up at Spunky's. That was home—we would start there and end up there. It was like we were celebrities. Everybody knew us. When we would go to Fairborn, whoever was there had to go. One time T-Bone and another guy were there. They tried to wait us out, but the girls made them leave. This went on for a while until I wrecked my Caddy. Then I took it as an omen and started pulling away.

Then it was January of 1983. We had pretty much stopped going to Fairborn and Pam and Jackie started chasing us down. Momma Hurt had a bootleg joint around the corner. All the neighborhood cats would be over there drinking and smoking weed. They would snort some blow every now and then. That is when I fucked up the party. I brought my test tube, some baking soda, some powder, and my pipe. They said, "What the hell are you doing?" I said, "Watch!" They sat around in amazement while I mixed up the concoction. I heated it and when it was finished, I shook it around and said, "Listen to this." *Tink. Tink.* "What the hell did you do?" they said!

Then out came the pipe and I let them check it out. Instantly I was the man. They came to me to cop what they wanted, paid me to cook it, and got me high.

In February of 1983, Gary and I went to a party in Fairborn with our girls. We had slipped away somehow. Then I saw this light-skinned, slim girl with a nice bubble butt go by. I noticed she had nice lips also. So I caught up with her and asked her name. "Donna," she said with a little feisty tone.

Hmm, attitude, I said to myself. *I like that.* She was going somewhere to the restroom, I thought. She was following her girlfriend. I can't remember who, but at any rate, she came back through and we had a brief conversation. She told me that she had seen me before at Spunky's. I found out that she had a daughter and she did hair. I said, "You do hair?" I said, "You think you could hook a brother up?" She said, "Sure," so I got her number.

So Gary and I kept our same routine—hitting the clubs and making money. At this time I was not really interested in finding a job. For one, we were having too much fun doing what we were doing. Plus, Gary and I were pursuing a musical career. A few weeks had passed and I had not called Donna. I found her number and I called her to see what she was doing. She said she was having a birthday party for her daughter. I asked if anyone there wanted to buy some weed; she asked a couple of the girls that were there. They said yes. She told me where she lived and told me to come on. Gary and I went over there and there was a house full of women, which made Gary happy. I was only interested in one, Donna. So we sold a couple of bags and on the way out I asked what they were doing after the birthday party. They said they were going to Spunky's. I said, "We might meet you there." Things seemed kind of cool. She had the cutest little girl—Jamaica is her name. I didn't know then, but she turned out to be one of the biggest joys of my life.

So as time went on, we talked a little more. I was just too busy to spend a lot of time with her. Between hustling, writing music, and practicing, that was all we could do. Gary and I used to hang out over at my cousin's house a lot. We would be from Town View to Summit Square sometimes a couple of times a day. I had cousins that lived in Town View and Summit Square. These were some of finest women in Dayton. But don't let the smooth stuff fool you. They had just as much game as some men I know, and would rumble too. It was Kim, Jackie, Sandy, and Bridgette. Betty was their mother. We all fell out of the same tree. Even though we weren't sister and brother, you sure couldn't tell.

So they told me that my uncle Sonny was having a party that night and asked Gary and me to come. Kim was kind of sweet on Gary. I think he was a little scared though—she was a little more aggressive than he was used to. So I called Donna and asked her if she wanted to go. She said sure, so Gary and I went and picked her up. Yes, me and Gary. You hardly saw one without the other. She had on a cute little outfit. I believe it was a plaid suede vest with a black suede miniskirt. For a skinny girl she had some strong-looking thighs and a nice ass.

We got to the party and I introduced her around. Everyone seemed to like her, but Sandy and the girls were checking her out closely. Later, Donna told me that Sandy told her, "Don't make me have to whip your ass about my cousin." Donna said she had never been so nervous in her life.

I told her, "That's just how my cousins look out for me." So we left and I took her home. I walked her to the door and kissed her good night. She had the softest lips. As time went on we grew closer. Gary and I would stop by sometime during the day every day. She told me it was hard for her mom to tell who she was going out with at first, because she would sit between us both. Then we would talk all night on the phone until we fell asleep.

It was now getting to be about April. Gary had dropped me off and went to Fairborn. Gary and his girl were still kicking it. Donna put Jamaica to bed. I don't know where her two younger sisters were—they were off somewhere. We went to the basement to listen to some music. As we were listening to music and looking at pictures, we started kissing. I started playing with her breast. I went for the left one because that seemed to be the favorite of a lot of women I had been with. At least, that's the one I had always got the most response out of. Then I unbuttoned her pants and slipped my hand in her panties and played with her clit while I was sucking on her nipple. I thought she came then by the way she was breathing and her body was flexing and squirming. That was one of my favorite things to do—watch women's reactions during foreplay. Then I slipped her panties off on my way to getting on my knees. Once on my knees, I slowly stuck my tongue in her vagina. I know she came then because I had to pull her back down on the couch. Then I started licking her clit real long and slow. Then I started sucking it and sticking my finger in her vagina and she came again. It was so thick and creamy. Then I gave her the dick. She really lost it then as I got more and more excited. She just kept on coming time after time. Her ass was slightly hanging off the couch. I was hitting it with long, slow, deep strokes. Man, that thing was just spitting and popping. It was so nice. When we finished, she said that was the best she ever had. In my mind I said it was the best I ever had also, but I wouldn't tell her that. I couldn't let her know that I was feeling a way about her already. As time went by we got closer and closer—nights of going out, making love, and spending days together.

It was now getting towards the end of April. Gary and I went to North Carolina to pick up my Buick. It was sweet—a '68 Buick Electra convertible, yellow and black, black leather interior, AC, and it was loaded. It was my dad's car at first; then he said that I could have it.

When we got back to Dayton, Donna had to go for a checkup. They found polyps on her uterus. They thought it was cancer. That is when I realized how much I cared for her. When we got that news, we held each other and cried like babies. It turned out to be nothing, which was a blessing. It was now May. The girl that I was seeing from Fairborn still couldn't get it in her head that our relationship was done. Gary and I were at the club; we met Donna and her cousin there. We were sitting at a table and the girl came over and offered us a drink. I turned it down. Then Donna invited her to the ladies' room. I wasn't in there, but I heard it wasn't pretty. We danced until it was time for the club to close, so we were leaving. Gary and I got in his car. Donna and her cousin got in her car and started out the parking lot. They were up the drive a bit; then the girl from Fairborn and her friend ran from around the building and jumped in the car with us. I was rolling a joint. This came as a surprise to me. Within seconds it seemed, Donna and her cousin pulled back around. Donna was talking shit. She said, "I don't have time to play these kind of games with you. Fuck you, Tim." So they left.

I told the girl from Fairborn, "You can't keep doing this." She apologized and gave me some head and Gary dropped me off at home. I ran in the house and called Donna to explain that I had nothing to do with that. This girl just didn't want to let go. Then out it came—"I love you, baby. All I want is you."

It got dead silent. She couldn't believe I said it and I couldn't either. She cried and said, "I love you too."

Time passed. It was now summer. In June or July Donna and I went to Spunky's. We danced and danced and danced. Everyone knew that we were in love. I used to just stare into her pretty brown eyes as we would slow dance. I would grab her ass and squeeze it. She would give me the biggest smile. We left Spunky's. I let the top down, put the boot over the top, and rode out. The night air was feeling especially good tonight. She loved riding with the top down. Anyway, we rode out into the country. I grew up out there, so I knew all kinds of spots. My favorite was the county pumping station. It had a long driveway that you could go down behind some trees. We pulled back there and parked and started kissing. I was rubbing on her favorite titty as I called it. Then I stuck my hand in her pants. As I was looking in her eyes, I pulled my hand out and sucked the juice off my finger. She gave me the biggest grin and said, "You are so nasty."

I said, "Yes, I am, but that's what you like about me." She said, "I know."

We got in the back seat. I was on my knees kissing her belly while she was standing on the seat. I got her pants down to her knees. I could see that muffin shining in the moonlight. I gently licked her clit and her knees buckled. I sat her on the back of the seat and went to work—sucking, fingering, licking, and kissing. She was so wet. We must have been out there for an hour. She would be sliding down on the trunk and I would pull her back up. I was really working it, doing that slow grind. As I started going deeper and faster, she started screaming, "Oh, baby. You're hitting it, you're hitting it." Then her body flexed real hard and started shuttering uncontrollably. As she was screaming, shit just went everywhere. Then we collapsed in each other's arms.

I said, "We'd better go before we fall asleep." I dropped her off at home, then went home myself. This was kind of strange to me, because I had women coming from everywhere and I was just not interested.

Time went on. It was August 1983 and I started thinking about a job. I got my resume together and within a couple of weeks I got a job, at Jeans West in the Salem Mall. It was in northwest Dayton. All the black people in Dayton shopped there. Well, maybe not all, but most of them were there at one time or another. This made it really hard to be faithful. Not only were these women pretty, but they had money too—plus all the women that worked in the mall.

Time moved on and things were good on the job, and I started running into some of my old street friends and met some new ones also. Pretty soon I had every kind of connection I wanted. I finally was making some decent money with my job and hustling combined. Before, just my hustling kept me living in my mom's house with all the other stuff I was paying for—like clothes, dining out, partying, and party supplies. Donna and I got our own apartment in November. It was government-subsidized projects basically. We had a lot of fun there. My cousins used to come through, and Gary was still around. My job was going strong and the hustle was even better. I was now selling as much coke as I did weed.

By the spring of 1985 I bought a Cadillac Seville. My brother was stationed at Fort Knox. I had a girl in Louisville that I had met when I went down with one of my partners. So I called her to see what was going on. I told her I had just bought a new car. She asked when I was coming down. I asked, "When do you want me to come?"

She said, "I really miss you. Can you come tonight?"

I said, "Let me get this new radio in and pack my clothes and I'll be there." I called Mike and told him about my car. I told him I was on my way to Louisville.

He said, "You're lying."

I said, "Nope, and I'll be there in a few hours." So Gary and I got finished with the radio, got my clothes, and went and got him some, and hit the road. We rolled into Louisville at about sundown. As we were riding down MLK, I saw a car make a U-turn behind us, and as they got closer they flashed their lights. It was my brother. When we stopped, he said that he had seen the Ohio tags. And it was a Seville. He said he knew it had to be me. We kicked it for a minute and I called my girl to let her know I had made it. She told me to go over to one of her friend's houses that lived in town and she would meet me there. Mike knew where it was at, so he led me over there. Gary got in the car with him and I said I would see them at the club later. I really wasn't feeling it at first, because I didn't know her. She could have been setting me up for a robbery or something. As I took my bath, I kept my nine close.

So my girl finally came. Damn, she was looking good. She gave me a big hug and kiss. I was, like, I guess you did miss me. We rode out, went and got some liquor, and it was off to the hotel. Robin was so fine. She was without a doubt one of the finest women I have ever been with. I was almost ready to leave Donna for her. She looked like a *Jet* centerfold. I mean, she had the total package. And she was intelligent also. And the sex was off the chain. That was some of that knock-your-ass-out sex—because afterwards I went straight to sleep. We didn't even make it to the club. The next morning I hooked up with my brother and got Gary and hit the road.

Shortly after we got back, I found out Donna was pregnant. We were so happy. We got married on July 6, 1985, to be exact. That was one big party. We got married at my mom's house. It was a small wedding with just a few close friends, and family members. We did not invite everyone to the wedding, because the house wouldn't hold everyone. The reception was off the hook. We rented a party room at Lakeview Estates; everyone was invited to that. We had so much food and liquor that everyone got full and drunk. It was so wild. The music was slammin'. My friend Rod had walked in the restroom on my mother-in-law; when she came out and as soon as she saw him, she slapped the fire out of him. My brother and his girlfriend were there and this dike—I don't remember who she came with but she was trying to pick up my brother's girlfriend. He went off. We had to carry him out. My wife and I had our first argument as we were leaving the reception and she wouldn't let me drive. She said I was too drunk; after a while I cooled down. After all, it's kind of pimpish to have your woman drive you around in your ride.

We got to Spunky's. It was off the hook. We had drinks coming from everywhere. They even had champagne for us. We were so in love. The DJ made the announcement that we had gotten married. A bunch of people congratulated us. But that still didn't stop the women from hitting on me. I kept my composure. Donna was getting a little heated. I had to tell I don't know how many people that I wasn't working. It's a shame that when people are trying to get high, they don't care what you have going on. We closed the club once again. When we got home, I was so drunk Donna had to push me up the stairs to keep me from falling back. Mike was trying to stay, but Darryl told him to come with him so that Donna and I could be alone. I guess he felt like he was losing his brother.

Before we got married, I had told Donna not to tell the neighbors in the apartments that we had gotten married, but what did she do? Donna went running her mouth, as usual. That was one of the complaints I always had, is that she talked too much. I knew they were going to tell, and sure enough, they did. The complex wanted to raise our rent. I said, "Hell, no." I wasn't going to pay five hundred dollars per month to live in the projects. We moved in with my mom for a while, which was cool because she could help Donna out. Besides, she was in that big house by herself.

I decided to leave Jeans West to make more money. I knew a couple of guys that worked for an electronics store. They made pretty good money, so I gave them my resume and went in and filled out an application and they hired me. I started at the warehouse store, but that didn't last long. I had gangsta parked my Seville out in the corner of the parking lot when the manager came into the morning meeting. He asked if that was my Caddy. I said yes. He asked if it got good mileage. I said yes. He said, "Good, because you are going to the Salem Avenue store." I was glad, because he seemed to be an asshole. I probably would not have lasted under him.

Things were going pretty good there. I was making good money and I was still hustling. I guess it was just in me to do that. December came and my little miracle came forth—my first baby boy. We named him Timothy II. He was about a month early and he had a few complications. He had inhaled some of his feces and they thought he might develop yellow jaundice. The doctors wouldn't let us take him home right away. The doctors had to do a spinal tap. It was so sad it made me cry. I had never felt that before. I made up in my mind that my family wouldn't want for anything. I turned up my game and went back to running women again.

About a month after I got married, I met a woman that owned a restaurant. She was fine as hell. She was thirteen years older than I was. She was about five foot seven, brown-skinned, and about 145 pounds, with the nicest ass you would want to see. But her owning a restaurant attracted me even more. I told her I was married, but that didn't seem to make a difference to her. She had bought a new house. When she took me to see it, we had sex all over that house before she had one piece of furniture in it—on the kitchen counter, on the steps, and everywhere. We left virtually no stone unturned.

As our relationship grew closer, it got to where I could get money and something to eat whenever I wanted. It got to where I was spending more time with her than I was at home. It started out as just having fun. I see now how you can have feelings for more than one woman. Her sex was so good—she was a real pro. Her stuff was so tight, even though she had three children. She never had natural childbirth; she always had C-sections. She said to me one night that she could make me cum whenever she wanted me to. I said, right. I thought I was the master of control. She got on top of me and started gyrating and riding up and down on my penis. And as if her stuff was not tight enough, she started flexing her muscles. It felt better than the best blowjob I ever had. It was like someone had put a spring in my back. I sprung up and wrapped my arms around her so she couldn't move. She said, "No, nigga. You're a bad-ass. Lay your ass back down." She pushed me down and went to work again. All of a sudden, my eyes rolled back in my head and I couldn't hold it anymore. I came so hard and she just kept going. I couldn't take it anymore. The feeling was so intense I pushed her off of me and she started laughing at me. She said, "I told your ass." Then we lay there and held each other.

I would go there and just relax. She used to ask me all the time, Why don't you stop hustling?—because she was afraid for my life, something Donna had never said. She didn't care about the money; she just wanted me. We would make love anywhere. We had sex at the restaurant, in her car, and all over the house. I had bought a brand-new Lynx XR-3 hatchback. We had gone somewhere and we got back to the house. I backed into the driveway. I got out to open the hatch. I had left the tape going. It was Sugar Foots' new tape. She used to love that. I let the back seat down flat and we climbed in. We made love right there in her driveway. She said, "Oooohhhhhhh, I like this." That was something that she had not done before.

Now I know why Tyrone Davis made that song: Trying to love two ain't easy to do. My feelings were getting stronger and stronger, as hers were also. It got to the point we would hold each other and cry when it was time for me to leave. I knew it was time to start pulling back. I said I would never leave my wife for another woman, but I could not let her go either. The only thing I liked better than her was my family and money.

In getting more into my hustle, it was also the start of my demise. Donna had a friend who had a boyfriend that was a hustler also. He and I hooked up, which turned out to be worse than the Oklahoma City experience. We had three rock houses; for a while it was fun. We had more than enough money to do what we wanted to do. Then all of a sudden it seemed that smoking was more important than making money. We were all headed downhill real fast. I would go to work from nine to nine, then run the streets all night. One time I got off work and went down to the house on Superior. When I knocked on the door, the police opened the door. They asked me what I was doing there I told them I saw my friend's car and I stopped to see if he was here. They said they didn't think I wanted to be there. I said, "I don't think I do either." I left and went to headquarters and called the other houses and told them to shut them down. I guess I got spooked.

One night, a guy we knew had an apartment on Kings Highway told us that we could bang out of his apartment. We put one of our boys in there. This worked pretty good for a while, until one morning when we went by to pick up our money we had to wake him up. We asked him where the money and the dope were. It turned out he had gotten robbed in his sleep. The person whose apartment it was, was there, so he had to know something. He swore he didn't. So we called our enforcer. If we had to kill somebody, we weren't going to do it ourselves. We had people to do that for us if it was to be done. Thank God, it never got to that. That's a whole other ball game there. When he got there, things got quiet. When someone walks in with a 357 in his hand, things would tend to get like that. We discussed what happened for a minute. Our boy said when he went to sleep, the dope was in a cigarette pack in his shirt pocket next to the money. Someone must have taken it out. Since it was our boy's responsibility, we made him do the deed, or take the bullet. Someone had traded some fishing poles for some dope. Our boy hit the dude in the jaw and knocked him in the corner, then whipped him with the fishing poles until he passed out. There was so much blood, screaming, and all kinds of commotion going on. My partner and I left before the police came.

Eventually, I left him alone. He always wanted to be so flamboyant, plus he was trying to play me the whole time. But how are you going to play a playa? Come to find out he was jealous of me the whole time. He hated my lifestyle and the fact that I was married and could do what I wanted to do. I had two cars; he was driving his girlfriend's car. All my children were with me. I also had a good job. I took my son to North Carolina for about four days. When I came back, he said to me in a nasty tone, "I wish I could take my son on a trip." The big difference was I also had a $35,000-a-year job. I wasn't just relying on the streets. While I was at work he was at home smoking up all the profits. Needless to say, I ended that relationship.

By this time I was getting pretty burnt out. All the working, hustling, getting high, and running women was getting to me. I was twenty-six and felt like I was twice that age. I was losing all kinds of weight. I figured out if I let my sales drop for a month or so, then Rex TV would fire me and I could get over four hundred dollars a week unemployment under the performance clause, so that's what I did.

Donna was pregnant with our second daughter, Antonia. I hung out with her and played with Jamaica and little Tim. In about May, I took off and went to North Carolina to hang out with my dad for a while. It felt good being in Carolina, especially that time of year—before it got too hot. Besides, I missed my dad. I would help him keep the grass cut. We would go to church and just kick it. It felt good not to have to do anything. I had my unemployment transferred, so I had money coming in. So all I had to do was chill.

Donna called and said she had the baby, so I went back to Dayton. She was already home when I got there. I went right to see her. She was so pretty, just like her dad, with one exception—she was brown-skinned. I said, "Donna, why is she so dark?" Donna and I were light-skinned and so were Jamaica and Tim. Then I had to think, my dad and my sister are brown-skinned and Mike was a little darker than me. I was the lightest one in my family. We named her Antonia Nicole, which was fitting, because she was so beautiful and she still is to this day. That is my chocolate, which all my children are beautiful. After Nikki was born, I hung out for a little while doing stuff around my mom's house and going down to my uncle's garage. I had little Tim with me most of the time; when he was not with me, everyone asked where he was. I wasn't really into a whole lot those days. This was about August 1987.

It was hot and steamy, and it was about time for me to get a job. I wasn't really hustling anymore—well, maybe a little bit. By now I had a nice little habit going on. I was drinking more and more. And every little bit of extra money I came across was going up in smoke. I had not totally lost control yet, but hold on.

I got a job at Larrick's Electronics. As usual, the Lord blessed me with a good income, a nice, clean job, and another chance at life— and what did my dumb ass do? It was not that I didn't love my wife and family, because I really did. Not only was I addicted to alcohol and drugs, but I was addicted to the lifestyle and everything that goes along with it—the women, the money, the cars, the clothes, and the power that came with them. My wife told me that she hated the way I could make people do what I wanted them to do.

It started off with the women. There was a Mexican girl that worked as a cashier. Man, she was fine, with big, pretty brown eyes; long, black, thick, curly hair; and a body. I always kept weed; she liked that. And she liked to drink. She tried to play hard at first, but that didn't last long.

We went out one night after work. We smoked a joint in the parking lot; then we went into the club. While we were sitting there having drinks, we made small talk—you know, the usual stuff about her family and my family; you know, normal stuff. Then the conversation got a little deeper, like, "What do you like in a man?" Then I turned the heat up a little. I went into what I used to call the Prince act—you know, sexy, not nasty, as I gently stroked her hand from her wrist down to her fingertips real slow and gentle, just so she could feel how soft my touch was. Then I told her how pretty and soft her skin was. Then I gently lifted her hand to my lips and kissed it—real soft and let it linger for a little bit. All the while I am waiting for a slow song.

So we were sitting and talking for a minute. I mean, I was putting it down. It was like I could see Olympic scorecard keepers in the background holding up 10s. Then a slow song came on and I asked if we could dance. We got out on the floor. Man, she felt so good in my arms. As I pulled her in tighter, I was talking real sweet and low in her ear. I felt her grip tighten up. She must have felt the bulge in my pants because she grinded on it a little bit. Then she caught herself and stopped. I heard a little tremble in her voice. Then I asked her if I could do something special for her. She rolled her head back and looked me in my eyes and asked, "What is that?" She already knew; she just wanted to hear me say it. Then I told her that I wanted to kiss her in her special place. Then she smiled. Women are just as nasty as men. They just try to hide it more.

We went outside and got in the car. She was all over me. I laid her back and pulled her panties down to her ankles. I put my lips firm on her clit then I gently sucked it with my tongue between my lips with soft, swift strokes. She came quicker than anyone I had ever seen. I was about ready to pull my pants down and let her get on top. Then a policeman drove through. So that was that. She had a man at home, so she felt kind of bad. She told me she had never done anything like that before. She just got caught up in the moment. We agreed just to be friends.

Then this sister came to work there. She was sexy too—a little different than what I was used to. She was short and chocolate, with long hair and a banging body. She had a tooth missing in the front, but that didn't mean anything, because she had such sexy mannerisms you would look past that. Plus she had money, and she didn't mind sharing. Actually, it was her husband's money, but I didn't care. She would get hotel rooms, and buy liquor and weed, which was cool because I was selling it. Even though we were sleeping together, that didn't mean anything. I still had to have my money. I had enough women to take care of—my wife, my mother, and my daughters. All the rest of them had to pay.

During our relationship, the two of them started getting close; that is, her and the Mexican chick. I was standing at the back of the show room putting some vacuum cleaners out. I looked up and they were at the cash register talking. They both looked at me and started talking again. I said, "Oh, shit. This doesn't look good." So the sister got with me later and asked me what was up with me and the Mexican chick. I told her that we hooked up once, but she wanted to be friends. "And since she saw you and I are kicking it, she is jealous."

She said, "Yeah, she sounded like it."

There was a guy that came to work there. He found out I sold weed and started buying weed from me. Then one day I was looking for something in the break room and happened to look behind a box on top of the refrigerator and found a little glass pipe—a crack pipe. I knew it could only be one person's. I asked the new guy if it was his. He said, "How did you know?" I told him that I didn't know anyone else there that got high or that would be into something like that. After that, he asked me if I knew where to cop.

I said, "Do I!"

So I hooked him up with my brother, because I was not really trying to get into the dope game, because of what I had been through. Besides, between my job and the women I was not doing bad. Plus I had the weed game on lock.

I had gone to Frank and J's and met this girl from Richmond Indiana. Her name was Katie. She was a little bigger than I was used to. But she was so sexy with it. She was about five foot ten and 160 pounds. Damn, she was juicy—nice breasts and a super-size ass and nice, big lips. She was so hot. When we would kiss I swear I believe she was coming right then. I mean, her knees would actually buckle. I mean, I thought I had to catch her from falling, and when we would make love she was so wet. She was wetter than anyone I had been with. She used to drive from Richmond to Centerville to pick me up. This was about seventy miles one way. She used to give just enough to keep me interested. She was trying to get me to leave my wife, and I explained to her that if I would leave my wife for her, what makes her think that I wouldn't leave her for someone else. So that relationship kind of went by the wayside. I was not mad, though. I was getting tired of going all the way to Richmond anyway. My addiction to crack was starting to get worse by now anyway. One night I was on my way to Richmond. I was smoking a premo. I ran out of dope by the time I got to her exit. So instead of going over to her house, I went back to Dayton and got some more dope. That was about thirty miles. That just goes to show how drugs can become more important than anything, including sex.

One night my brothers and I were hanging out at the fox. G-man had been my barber since I was ten years old. He always kept me fresh. Every time I would get my hair cut, I could go anywhere and cats would say, "You've been to Creative Cut, haven't you?" All the barbers there had a certain flair about them. To this day Carl, Joe, and G-man are still holding it down. Anyway, we were out kicking it. This girl came out of nowhere and asked me to dance with her. We introduced ourselves and hit the floor. Her name was Shandra. She wasn't a real pretty girl, but she had a real athletic look about her. She just looked real strong, with nice, firm breasts, strong legs, and kind of tall too. So as we danced we got more acquainted. She was very aggressive. It was kind of refreshing at first, but after a while it started to get on my nerves. I found out that she liked to get high. I knew that would be another source of income. She had a couple of other girls with her.

After we left the club they were parked over by some bushes. We sat out there and talked, drank, and tooted a little until almost four in the morning. My barber still teases me about it to this day. He'll say, "Tim, you remember that night we were in the bushes?" And I know exactly what he's talking about.

I went back to work on Saturday. There was a new girl that started working there named Tosha. She was fine also—kind of short, but she had some big boobs, and nice, little, tight butt. She was young also. The main thing she had going for her was her little red sports car.

As time went on we got closer. She used to let me drive her car all the time. I liked that because it kept my car from getting hot. That was the closest I ever came to getting busted for being with another woman. The sex was OK, but the lack of money made it less appealing.

In the meantime I got promoted to store manager at the Macoil Streetstore. Things got a lot better on my job. It made it easier for me and Shandra to get together, because she lived in Xenia and the store was off of I-35. She would call and say she needed a package. I would meet her somewhere near the store and take care of business. Then I would go to Xenia sometimes and take care of her and her friends. When I would go up there, I would always end up in bed with her. But that was getting pretty old, because instead of letting things happen, she was getting real demanding.

One weekend she asked me to go out of town with her. She was going to a wedding in Saginaw, Michigan. I told her that my brothers Mike and Randy were going to North Carolina to see my dad that weekend and I was planning on going with them. She said if I went with her we could meet there. So I took off work for a week. I told Donna that I was going on a run with one of my cats. This was nothing strange.

So we left on a Friday and got to Saginaw that night. We checked in the hotel and went and kicked it with some of her friends. Then we went back to the room and smoked some weed and did a few lines. And you know what happened next? Yes, we had sex. The next morning we started to get dressed. I pulled out my bag and she told me to put it up. She said, "Here I had wondered what all the bags were." She had bought me all kinds of clothes—shorts sets, jeans, sneakers, T-shirts, dress slacks, and all kinds of stuff.

I immediately thought, *I can't take all this home.* I said, "I know what I'll do. I'll give some to my brother when we get to Carolina." So I thanked her with some more dick.

So we went to the wedding and reception. It was nice. We didn't go to the after-party, because we had to get up in the morning to head out for North Carolina. We retired and had sex again. It seemed like all we did was drive and have sex all weekend. So we got up the next morning and left Michigan for North Carolina. I didn't go back the way I would normally go as if I was going from Dayton. I could have gone back through Dayton, but I wanted to see some new scenery. So we took the Ohio Turnpike across to 77 and went straight to Carolina. I turned a thirteen-hour trip into about a ten-and-a-half-hour trip. I was putting it down, because one of my favorite things to do besides getting high and having sex was driving. So we got to North Carolina and checked in a hotel and went over to my dad's house. We kicked it for a little while; then we went and got something to eat. Then we went to Charlotte to go out. We had a good time, but I was so tired from the trip we didn't stay out long. We left and went back to the hotel. We stayed about four days and came back home.

We got home—well, back in Ohio, anyway. She lived in Xenia and I lived in Dayton. So we went to her house. I kissed her goodbye and got in my car. She walked over to my car. I rolled the window down. She reached in her purse and pulled out a bank envelope. She said, "I forgot to give you this." Then she said, "Thanks for such a good time." I opened the envelope and there was $350 in it. I pulled away from the house.

I thought in my mind, *Now that's pimpin'*. So I got to Dayton. The first stop was my brother's house. I stopped to give him some of the clothes that I got. I knew that I couldn't take all that stuff home without a million questions. When I got home, I put my clothes away and played with my children for a while. Then I gave Donna some money and took everyone out to eat.

So I guess you would say by now, how can I say I loved my wife and children by the way I was carrying on. But refer back to the beginning and remember the way I was brought up. You'll see that my behavior was bred into me way before the first drink or the first drug. As you will see later in the book, it would take a lot of years and a lot of turmoil and a lot of God to break this cycle.

Well, I'll go back to the drama. It was 1989. I was twenty-nine. My money was progressing and so was my addiction. Larrick's had gone out of business, so I decided to hustle full time—and I did pretty well, I might add. All my sales experience and street skills together made me lethal. If I could have kept the drugs out of me, I could have been the greatest. But I guess that is not what God had for me. I really knew people and I could get just about anyone to do anything I wanted.

One week one of my partners asked me to go to Chicago with him and a couple of his cats. We were going to get some goods. We had about thirty-five thousand dollars and some change between all four of us. We left on a Wednesday night. We stopped in Indianapolis and bought a case of Schlitz malt liquor. Then we continued on to Chicago. We were drinking, smoking, and talking trash. We were having big fun.

So we got to Chicago and checked into the downtown Marriot. I had the bag with the rest of the beer in it. We were standing in the lobby of the Marriot, and the bottom of the bag broke. There were beer cans rolling all over the floor. It was so embarrassing. It cost us $450 for two rooms for one night. The next day we checked out because we thought we were going to hook up with his people. We waited all day and nothing happened. So we checked into another hotel across town. After running around all day, we were kind of tired. So we crashed. The next morning I woke up early and went to Burger King to get some breakfast. There was a young cat there kicking it with the other employees; he was also an employee. He had a little gold chain on and he had kind of a thuggish appeal. So I figured he might know something. So I said to him, "Come here." He came over and sat down. I asked him if he knew how to bake a cake. Oh, by the way, "cake" is slang for kilo. So he sat back and looked at me like he was unsure what to say. I told him that I and some of my boys came up from Dayton to hook up. But their people couldn't do anything. I told him we were staying across the street at the hotel. I gave him the room number and told him to call me if he could come up with something.

So I went back to the room and told my partner Derek I had us hooked up. They laughed and said, "You ain't done shit." So I lay down and went to sleep. The phone rang about 1:00 p.m. Derek said, "Telephone, Tim," so answered it. It was my cat I met at Burger King. He gave me directions to go see this one cat on the other side of town. He was from Cleveland; we found that out while we were sittin' there chillin'.

So we kicked it with him for about an hour or two, smoking weed and drinking. I guess he was checking us out. Believe me, we were checking him out too. So after a while he said, "Let me go make a call." When he came back out, he told us to follow him. So we did. In the dope game, all you got to rely on is instinct, because it doesn't matter if you know them or not. Always expect the unexpected and stay strapped. We all were packing heat, so it didn't matter. So he took us over to another part of Chicago. It was a nice little subdivision. Things were looking up. I started to feel a little more at ease. We parked and went in. Come to find out we were at a famous athlete's dad's house. We met up with his little brother. He made a phone call. And to make a long story short, we left with a half a bird. By the way, "bird" is slang for kilo also and we had no drama. It was even dropped off by a guy in a city dump truck.

So we got back to Dayton. It seems after that little trip, it sky-rocketed me into greater street fame. They had told all the hustlers what I pulled off in Chi Town. For months all I heard was, "Damn, Tim, that was some fly shit." So I felt like I had arrived. Not only did I have a wife and three beautiful children, I was a master of the dope game. Plus I had a boatload of women. I had money coming from everywhere.

I was really caught up in the game by now. I really had it going on. I had a really good street rep now. I was doing a lot of business, and it seemed I was able to have any woman I wanted. One night, a friend and I had some girls over at his house. The intent was to have an orgy, but it didn't go down like that. We were all naked and smoking dope. I got in the bed with my girl; his girl tried to get him in the bed. But all he wanted to do was smoke, so you know what my greedy ass did? That's right, I did both of them, and got them off too. You know, it's a shame when you've been with so many women you can't remember their names. And I really wouldn't even know some of them if they were staring me right in my face. I pray that God forgives me.

Now the guy I turned my brother on to had called; he said he didn't like dealing with Mike. He said he was always late and when he would get there he would talk crazy to him, so he asked if he could just deal with me. So I started taking care of him myself.

Time went on. My cat was getting bigger. Guess what happened to me—I grew right with him. B was a white guy, if you remember. I worked with him at Larrick's. He was kind of cool though. I say "kind of" because I didn't really trust him all that much. I trusted him enough to sell him something. But I would never, ever front him anything.

I used to love going over to his house; you just never knew what would be going on. Bryan had a wild-ass girlfriend. She had a lot of stripper girlfriends; most of them were white girls with nasty-ass attitudes. And they really didn't like black people too much. Her girlfriends used to say shit like, "You look good for a black guy." What kind of shit is that? So one night I went over and it was a black girl over there—I mean, she was black as night and pretty as hell with a bangin' body. The only thing I didn't like was that fake-ass hair. I couldn't stand to feel it on my skin. B's girl introduced us. But I can't remember her name for the life of me. The sex was OK and the head was even better. I wasn't really all that interested, because one thing I know about strippers is that they like to get money. They're not into givin' it up. So with me it was M.O.B. every day, all day. So needless to say, I didn't mess with her long.

As time went on, B built up to about one-fourth bird a week. With my other two main customers, I was knocking down about one-half bird a week. I used to sell hundred-dollar blocks to dope houses; that was a lot safer than sitting in them.

I used to have different people ride me around so my car wouldn't get hot. One night one of my cats took me to a house on Mia Avenue. It was about five degrees outside. When we came back out, his car wouldn't start, so were standing there with the hood up and the police came down the street. He stopped and I said to myself, *Oh, shit.*

He said, "Are you having car problems?" We said yes. He said, "There is a phone book down at the end of street. Do you have someone you can call?" I said yes. He said, "Get in the back and I'll give you a ride down there." Now, mind you, I had a half ounce of rock cocaine in my underwear. On the way down to the phone booth, he said, "What happened? Your car won't start?"

I said, "No, we were coming down the street and it stopped."

He said, "This is a bad place for your car to stop."

I said, "Yeah, I know." So I called over to my house and told Donna to come and get us. He took me back up to the car and let me out.

Then he said, "Be careful, and have a good night." When he left we waited until he was out of sight. We went back in the house and got high some more within about ten minutes. Donna had sent one of her girls to get us.

As time went on, my addiction got stronger and stronger. Everywhere I went, I would smoke some dope. I would go from dope house to dope house. Every time I would sell some, I was taking a hit. I started to notice the people I was selling to looking at me strange. But I didn't pay it.

My brother and Gary had gone down to North Carolina. We used to go down there and take product from time to time. I and one of the guys I grew up with were out riding around taking care of some business. I had hit a nice little lick. I asked him if he wanted to go to North Carolina; he said yes and we could drive his car. He had a new Toyota Corolla. I knew it would be great on gas. I called

Donna and told her to get my clothes ready. I went home, took a nap, and had a little sex. By that time Rod had pulled up. I left Donna some money and some dope. Oh, I didn't tell you she was smoking too. I went and made a couple moves before we left. I had one-fourth ounce. I had cooked one-half of it and put it in my cigarette pack. I put the other 8 ball of powder in my draws.

We got down to the bridge going across to Kentucky. I had rolled a primo. We smoked it and I went to sleep. When I woke up and looked at the sign, we were just getting to Lexington. I had been asleep for over two hours. I knew it should have only taken about an hour. I said, "Man! What have you been doing?"He said, "Driving."

I reached for a cigarette. I had put them in the cup holder before I went to sleep. But now they were gone. I asked him what happened to them. He said, "Look in the trunk."

I said, "Why in the hell would I put my cigarettes in the trunk?"

We were too far out of town for me to do anything. Plus we were in his car. Besides, everyone knew we left together. So he had just beaten me out of an 8 ball. It was everything I could do to keep from throwing him over one of those mountains.

When we got to Knoxville, I went to Kroger. I bought a metal measuring spoon and some baking soda. I stopped at the gas station and got some ice water. I pulled the 8 ball of powder out of my draws. I put a little in the spoon with some baking soda and cooked another rock while we were riding down I-40. I rolled a joint. He said, "You aren't going to give me any?"

I said, "You got an 8 ball. Smoke that."

He said, "I'll turn around and go back."

I said, "Go ahead. You don't have any money. Wherever we run out gas, that's just where I'm going to leave you." So we kept forward to North Carolina. So he started getting tired and I made him let me drive. I was going about eighty through the mountains.

He said, "What are you trying to do—kill us?"

I asked him, "Can you think of anyone better to die with?" He was scared senseless. I was trying blow his engine, but I backed off because were in the mountains. And I didn't want to have to get out and walk. So we got to Kings Mountain. I told my brother what happened. He just shook his head.

We had big fun down there—going out to eat, going to clubs. Man, we had all the women. I gave Rod hell all the while we were there. Mike asked me why I was doing Rod like that. I said, "I'm not feeding him shit. He shouldn't have stole from me. If you want him to eat, you feed. He's lucky I don't leave his black ass down here."

We left North Carolina on Sunday. After we left the Hungry Fisherman, we were rolling. I think it only took about seven hours to get home. Normally it takes about eight to eight and a half. When we got home, Donna had gone to work, so I went to sleep. B called me about 1:00 p.m. He said the wanted a quarter and an eighth of a bird. I said, "Cool." Just to give you an idea of the money I was going to make, the total package cost me $10,000. I charged him $14,500. Now that's pimpin'. Donna came home during the transaction and freaked out. She had never seen that much money and dope at one time. She was raising so much hell I gave her $1,200 and told her to go shopping. This quieted her down real quick. She said OK and took the kids and left.

It was now getting to be where I was blowing more money than I was making. I had about five girlfriends outside my marriage, and the funny part is all of them thought the other one was just a customer. One time Donna came home from work and three were there waiting on me to get back from making a run. They were cleaning my house, playing with the kids, even starting dinner for me. Even though I was doing what I did, I still made sure my babies were OK.

In 1989 one of the big guys in Dayton got busted. That messed it up for everyone for a long time. There were a bunch of murders going on; people were getting popped left and right. I guess it was just bad luck everywhere. My addiction was in full swing also, and to top it off, Donna was pregnant. On top of that, I wrecked my Lincoln and lost my house. My life was going to hell in a hand basket. It was slipping away so fast I couldn't grasp hold to anything.

So in about February or March I had moved in with Terry. Donna had moved back to her mom's. We were both so screwed up on drugs by this time, we weren't any good to ourselves, let alone each other. I had bought a little Chevette from a guy that used to buy dope from me. That was my only transportation.

Terry and I weren't any better. She had a decent job and the sex was good. I mean, she liked everything—even anal sex. I wasn't crazy about it. But I aim to please; whatever a woman wants, she's got it. It had come to the point I had her doing tricks with her bank card. We would make a fake deposit at one bank machine at 11:45 p.m. and then withdraw it at a few minutes after 12 a.m. We did it so much the bank cancelled her card and pressed charges, which messed things up since she worked for the courts.

Donna and Terry had become friends. She really didn't know what kind of relationship Terry and I had. Donna talked Terry into letting her move in. A couple of the guys that used to cop from me would come by and see Donna sitting with me and Terry and trip. They started calling me Goldie after the Mack. It was fun for a while. But it soon played out. Donna would go to work and Terry and I would have sex, and at night Donna and I would sleep together. There wasn't any sex going on at this time, because she was going to have the baby in a month or so. I was uncertain as to what was going to happen with the baby. I would try to get her to stop using. The more I would try, the angrier she would get with me. That goes to show how sick addiction is, even though you know you're losing everything, or even stand the chance of losing a baby. Nothing mattered but the drugs.

So I called myself trying to get away. That didn't work either. I went to North Carolina, back to my dad's house. I ended up getting a job at Hardee's. Now here I am a grown man, working at Hardee's. I went from making forty to fifty thousand dollars a year to working at Hardee's.

This time Carolina was different. I wasn't selling dope. I was using every chance I got and my drinking had gotten worse also. I was high or drunk every day. Barry and I went out one weekend to a club in Charlotte; that's where I met Lory. Barry and I were sitting across the club. I noticed this young lady across the club staring at me. So I got up and went and talked to her. I introduced myself. I said, "Hi. My name is Tim." She said, "Hi. I'm Lory."

I said, "It's nice to meet you."

She was dark-skinned and smooth as silk. She was beautiful—long hair, the works. She told me that she and her girlfriend came down from Statesville to come to the club. I asked her how far Statesville was from Charlotte. She said about fifty miles. So we danced a little and sat and talked for a bit. I couldn't keep my eyes off of her. Soon it was time to go. I walked her to her car, got her number, and said good night.

This turned out to be pretty nice for a while. I would go and see her and she would come and see me. Her mom sold moonshine, and she would bring me some every time she came down. We spent a lot of time together. One weekend she came to see me. I was sitting across from her just looking at her, she was so beautiful. We were sitting there quiet just looking at each other. I noticed her lip was twitching. I said to myself, *This bitch is crazy.* Sure enough it came out. One day I had bought a pint of liquor. She took me to work. When she picked me up, she told me she and my dad had a few drinks, but they saved me some. When I looked at it, it was only about half a shot. So I told her to go ahead and drink the rest, and I would go up to the bootleggers and get some corn liquor. So I left. When I got back, her hatch was up on her car. I said to myself, *What the hell is going on here?* So I went into the house and noticed her curling irons on the coffee table. I asked her what was going on. She said, "Tim, if you wanted me to leave, you could have told me."

I said "What?"

She said, "You didn't have to put my clothes in the car." I told her I didn't touch her clothes. I just got back from up the street. She said, "Yes, you did. You even put my curling irons on the table."

I said, "Girl, you have got a problem." What did I say that for? She jumped up in chest and went off. I called her mom to ask what was wrong with her.

She said, "Tim, has Lory been drinking?" I said yes. She said, "Whatever you do, please don't let her get on that highway."

I said, "She's going to have to get the hell out of here." Then Lory started on me again. She calmed down after a while. Then she apologized and we had sex like there was no tomorrow. I really liked her, but soon my past caught up with me.

One weekend Terry said her and another girlfriend of ours were coming down. I didn't believe they were coming. Sure enough, Lory and I were lying in bed one Saturday morning when there was a knock at the door. I got up to see who it was. When I looked out of the door, my son was standing there. Terry and Dee had come down and brought my son and her son with them. I told Lory to get up and I let them in. Terry was heartbroken. She had tears in her eyes. She got on the phone and called Donna and told her I was there with another woman. She said, "Donna, she is beautiful too." So I had to get on the phone and argue with her. So Lory left and I had to stay there and deal with this bull. Needless to say, it was a very tense weekend.

Soon I realized I couldn't run from myself, so I saved enough money for a bus ticket back to Dayton. I ended up staying wherever I could—sometimes at my mom's, or over at Terry's. So Donna had the baby. Thank God there wasn't anything wrong with him. All I wanted to do was get high. Donna came home from the hospital and I was back to my same old stuff—trying to hustle, not realizing all I was doing at this point was hustling myself. I finally got tired of all the getting high, all the arguing, all the trickery, and finding ways and means to get more dope. I really hated what I had become. I finally checked myself in for rehab. This was a thirty-day program. I was really hoping that this would do it. What I didn't realize is that I had to change more than just the using dope. I had to change my attitude and my behavior.

After a week or so, I had forgotten about the pain I had that had caused me to check myself into treatment in the first place. I was sitting around telling war stories, acting like I was such a big shot—talking about how much money I had made, remembering only the good times, forgetting all about how cocaine had kicked my ass. I even had sex with a patient in my bathroom. God was giving me another chance and I was throwing it back in his face. After thirty days, Donna came and picked me up and we went straight to the dope house.

By this time Terry had lost her house and job, so we all were homeless. Donna went to her mom's. I stayed between there and my mom's. I did that so I could still have freedom. I kept getting high for about a month and a half. One night, Terry and I were in her mom's basement. We had just finished getting high and having sex. I was lying there geeking. I started thinking about robbing something to get some more dope. I said to myself, *This is crazy. I've never had to rob anything in my life.* The next day I checked myself right back in for treatment. This time I was a little more serious. The pain had gotten so great, after only being out of treatment for a month and a half, I was going crazy. So I told them that if I was going to stay clean, they were going to have to get me out of Dayton, and that's what they did. They got me a bed at the Salvation Army in Cincinnati.

This was November of 1990. This was the first time I remember being away from my family on Thanksgiving. That really hurt me. I would wake up in my room and look around and realize I was sleeping in a room with eight other men. I said to myself, *How the hell did I get here?* I was ready to try anything after being robbed and held hostage. That's right—held hostage. One time I had put a drug deal together. It was me and a couple of other people. I went through someone else and his boy ran off with the money. So they thought I had something to do with it. He ran off with my money too. In a day or so, they came over to Terry's and I left with them to go find out what happened. As we were riding down Gettysburg, this chick was laid back in the seat hitting a stem. I said, "Instead of smoking, let's go sell some of that shit so we can get back." We ended up back at her house. We were sitting there getting high when her brother pulled out a gun and put me and the guy that helped me put the deal together in the basement. They tied us up and went back upstairs and continued getting high. At about three o'clock in the morning they ran out of dope. I knew they would. I also knew they would be going to get some more. When I heard the car hit the driveway, I got myself untied and got out of the basement window and ran around to my mother-in-law's house and went to sleep. That's when I decided to check myself into rehab the first time.

Now I'm in Cincinnati at the Salvation Army in a ninety-day program. It's all men, so all I could do is focus on my recovery. I started going to NA meetings. That's when my attitude started changing. I was finally getting it. That's when I heard it—if the drugs don't get you, the lifestyle will. When I got out of the Salvation Army, I had made up my mind to stay in Cincinnati. I never had been scared to try something new before. Terry would come and see me sometimes. I think this gave her the inspiration to get clean. This one time she came to see me, we went back to Dayton. I was driving up I-75 and she was giving me a blowjob when we had a blowout. She stopped sucking it for a minute. She said, "We had a blowout." I told her not to worry about it and to keep doing what she was doing. She started working on it again. I eased over on the shoulder of the road close to an exit ramp. She went up and down, and around and around on it. I had another blowout. Then I slowly drove off the ramp and got a tire.

My brother Mike let me use one of his cars to get back to Cincinnati. I kept his car for a while until I could get my own, which didn't take long. As time went on, I had been to I don't know how many NA meetings, and the message was starting to sink in. The message was that anyone could stop using, and lose the desire to use, and find a new way to live as long as you follow their way. So that's what I did and I started feeling better and better about myself.

After a couple of months I got a job at Circuit City. This would turn out to be the best job I ever had. I was honest with them. I told the manager I was in recovery and I needed time to go to meetings. They were so impressed with my resume and my honesty that they hired me on the spot. Right then I knew that God was looking out for me.

After a couple of weeks, they flew me to Richmond, Virginia, for training. This was a blast. I was thirty-one years old and this was my first time flying. I was a little nervous but I made it through, and I did it sober. I got to Richmond and checked into the hotel. This was pretty sweet. I really felt like an executive and I was fresh out of treatment. I really felt God working in my life. We would go to meetings in the day and clubbing at night. They had an area in Richmond called the Chocko Slip or something like that. My second night out I met Sherry. We danced and kicked it all night. I really started to like her; truthfully, I wanted to do her. That was an addiction that hadn't gone anywhere yet. It felt kind of strange being in a club and not drinking. I met a guy from Morocco. I was talking to him for a while. He worked for Sun Oil. I told him I was in town with Circuit City and I told him about Sherry. He told me Sun Oil had gotten him two rooms and I could stay in one of them if I wanted to. I told him thanks, but I had to get back to work.

Training went well. I got back to Cincinnati. I had my own apartment by now. I remembered that I went out in Richmond and I didn't drink. So I figured I could do it now. I went to a club called Brandy's. I would drink cranberry and orange juice. I met a girl named Mary. We talked for a while and danced a little bit. She asked me what I was drinking and I told her. She said, "You don't drink alcohol?"

I said, "Not today." I found out she was an electrical contractor, and there I go again—seeing dollar signs. This made me even more interested. She told me she had an office in Mount Auburn that overlooked downtown Cincinnati. She asked me if I wanted to see it. I said sure. I was almost embarrassed to let her see this raggedy-ass Lincoln I was driving. She never even mentioned it. That made me feel good. That meant that she wasn't interested in what I was driving.

We got to her office and went up to the top floor. It seemed like a million steps. I asked, "Why didn't we take the elevator?" She laughed as she showed me around. She fixed herself a drink and fired up a joint. I noticed that I didn't have a desire to partake. I thanked God. I was looking out the window. This was the first time I had seen Cincinnati like this. It was beautiful and I was still clean. She moved over next to me after she put the joint out. We started kissing. I didn't like the taste of the alcohol and the weed, but my dick was hard. I started unbuttoning her blouse. I slowly worked my way down her neck. She started breathing a little heavy and didn't say stop, so I continued. By this time we were sitting in the window sill. Soon I had her bra loose. I was sucking and nibbling on her breast. I would go back and forth to see which one I got the most response out of. It was the right one. This was really beautiful. While I was sucking and licking on her breast, the moon was shining so big and bright, it made the wetness on her nipples shine like a streetlight. She had on a miniskirt. I gently raised it and started slipping her panties down. Again she didn't say stop, so I didn't. I laid her back in the window sill and opened her legs. Her vagina was so wet it was shining in the moonlight like a neon sign that said eat me. So I did; she had the biggest clit I had ever seen. I put my lips gently around it and stroked it lightly with my tongue. I thought she was going to jump out of the window. She started twisting and flexing and moaning and groaning as I slid my tongue ever so gently and slowly around her clit. It looked like it had gotten bigger. As I slowly slid my tongue in and out of her vagina, I ran it back up to her clit. Now there was a little stream coming out of her vagina down between her cheeks. As I sucked on her clit, her body was starting to tremble. I stuck my finger in her vagina and played with that little spot on the inside right behind the clit. She grabbed me by the back of my head and pulled my face into her vagina as hard as she could, then she let out the loudest scream I ever heard. Suddenly as her body tensed, I felt wetness on my hand all the way to my wrist. Then she practically slammed me on the ground and unzipped my pants and pulled them down. She jumped on top of me and started riding me like there was no tomorrow. I was so excited, I came in about two minutes. She collapsed on top of me. I tried to explain to her that I hadn't been with a woman in about a month or two and that's why I got off so quick. She covered my mouth and said that was OK, because she had never come like that in her life.

The next morning I got up to go to work. She called at about ten o'clock and asked what I was doing when I got off work. I told her I had to go to a meeting. She said, "A meeting?"

I said, "Yeah, a meeting." She wanted to know what kind of meeting. I explained that I went to NA meetings. She said, "No wonder you weren't smoking or drinking." She also said she liked that in me and apologized for doing it in front of me. Then she said, "Can I see you after the meeting?" I told her I would call her after the meeting. I knew that as much as I liked sex, cocaine had whipped my ass so bad I wouldn't dare miss a meeting.

So after the meeting I called like I said I would. She asked me to come over for something to eat. It felt so good to be able to kick it without drugs and alcohol. We ate and talked for a minute. I had to be at work early; besides, I was really enjoying having my own apartment. Time went on and we got a little closer. I could see things were starting to change. She was starting to monopolize my time, so I started slacking off a bit.

By now Mike was crying about his car, so I started looking for a car. My credit was torn up, so I didn't know how I was going to do it. I went to Thomson-McConnell Cadillac. I found an Olds 98; it was a 1979, powder blue. It wasn't the cleanest car I'd ever had, but it was better than what I was driving. They wanted me to put some money down or get a cosigner first. So I went to Mary's and showed her the car. I told her what I needed; she said she would do it for me. I said, "Cool," so we went back to the dealership, signed the paperwork, and rode off into the sunset. Later on, I thanked her for helping me.

The next weekend or so, I went to Dayton to see my children and give Donna some money. Donna and my ex-sister-in-law were living together at that time. Donna and I left and went to the store. I got out and went in; when I got back to the car she had gone through my glove box. She said, "I see you are up to your old tricks again."

I said, "What are you talking about?"

She said, "Who is Mary?" She said she had seen her name on the bill of sale.

I told her, "Don't worry about it. I had to do what I had to do. Besides, you couldn't help me. Stay out of my business." We went back to the house. I went in and kissed my babies goodbye and went back to the Nati.

A few weeks later, I figured it was time to put it on the road. It had done OK going back and forth to work and up to Dayton. Sherry and I had been keeping in touch, so I took off and drove to Richmond, Virginia. I got there and called her. She was living with her parents at the time. She told me how to get out there; I went and picked her up and we went to a movie and dinner. Then we went and got a room. I had planned to stay the weekend. But she said she had some other stuff to do. We spent the night together. The sex was OK. I guess I was just tired; it wasn't one of my best performances. We got up the next morning and went and ate breakfast; then I went to get a car wash and went to North Carolina.

When I got to my dad's house, his eyes lit up. He was so happy to see me cleaned up. He hadn't seen me sober in a while. It really made me feel good to see him. And finally he didn't have the look of disappointment. My dad has always been my hero. He had a lot going for him. He only went to the eighth grade in school. He was as successful as anyone I knew. He was a supervisor at Dayton Coca-Cola Bottling Company; plus he had his own trucking business. All the women loved him.

Meanwhile back at the ranch, my workweek started as usual. Maggie and I were standing at the counter talking. She said she had someone she wanted me to meet. I said, "Oh, yeah?"

She said, "Yeah." I asked her what she looked like. She said she was nice-looking and was sweet too. I told her to call her for me. She did, we talked for a few minutes, and I invited her to lunch. She said that she would come out one day.

I said, "Cool."

She sounded really nice on the phone, but I was always skeptical of that. Normally when they sound real nice on the phone, they aren't much to look at. In the meantime, Mary was starting to nut up on me. I mean, she wanted to see me all the time. She even wanted me to give her a key to my car. I said that wasn't going to happen. Trick no good. She got upset with me and said that she didn't have to cosign. I told her to start helping me with payments and she could have all the keys she wanted. That went over like a fart in a space suit.

After a few days, I talked to Maggie's friend again; her name is Darla. I asked her, "What about lunch Saturday?" She said OK. Saturday came; it had to be about eleven or twelve o'clock when she walked back to see Maggie. Then Maggie came out with her and introduced us. The first thing I noticed was her big, brown, almond-shaped eyes and her big, juicy lips. Damn, she was sexy. Darla was about five foot seven with a slender build. We stood and talked for a minute. I asked what she wanted for lunch. She said she didn't care. I told her I had to go to the back for a minute, and that she could wait in the stereo department if she wanted and I would be right back with her. When she turned to walk, I noticed that nice, round bubble and those sexy legs. She had some strong-looking calves.

We went to Frisch's—not overly expensive but not cheap either. I wanted to make a good impression, but not spend a bunch of money. Besides, I didn't even know if I liked her or not. As we ate and talked, she had a classiness about her that I liked. You know—just enough, not real prim and proper. She seemed like the kind of woman that was real sweet but would go there with you if provoked. We talked about what was going on with each other. I found out she had two daughters and was divorced. She had her own car and a decent job. She was an independent girl. That was a plus. She asked if what I was eating tasted good. I replied, "Yes, but probably not half as good as you." She sat back and gave me a look like, here we go. I immediately apologized to her. I thought I had screwed up.

I went back to work and she went her way. She gave me her number and told me to call her later, so I guess I didn't do too bad. I called her a couple of times. Sometimes I would say little suggestive comments and she would laugh and say, "You are nasty." I told her in time that would probably be one of the things she liked about me. A couple of weeks later, she told me that her daughters were going to their dad's for the weekend. I was like, "Oh yeah?" I asked her if she wanted to go out. She said sure.

I picked her up. She had on a form-fitting shirt and a miniskirt with some pumps. Not real sleazy but very seductive. She had a lot of class, so I, being the perfect gentleman that I was, said, "Damn, baby, you look good." We walked to the car. I opened the door for her—I mean, I was really turning it on. We went to Brandy's and went in and got a seat. The waitress came over. She ordered wine and I had my usual cranberry and orange juice. She said, "Why aren't you drinking? Are you planning to take advantage of me?"

I said, "No, of course not." I explained to her that I was in recovery. I mean, I told her everything.

She seemed almost spellbound that I was being so honest with her. Then she said, "Let's dance."

Luther was on. I was like, "Oh, shit."

We got up to dance. As I was holding her, I was looking in her eyes talking big shit. I gave her a little peck on the lips. She laid her head on my shoulder and said, "Damn, you smell good." As we danced, there was a little swelling going on in my pants. She looked at me and smiled and said, "Is something wrong?"

I was a little embarrassed. I said, "I'm sorry. You just feel so good in my arms; plus it's been so long since I held a woman like this."

We were on our way back to her house. She said, "I really enjoyed myself." I said, "So did I." When I walked her to the door, she asked if I wanted to come in for a minute. Then came the words, "I'd love to."

She said, "Have a seat. I'm going to get comfortable."

Not to sound too anxious, I said, "OK.". She came back after a minute. I mean, she took a shower and everything. She had on a silk robe and some kind of sweet fragrance. I don't know what it was—all I know is that I liked it. She even had pretty feet. It was hard, but I was still trying to be on my best behavior. She was a little different than what I had been used to, and besides, she was a friend of a coworker. I really didn't want to do anything wrong.

She asked me if I wanted some juice or something before she sat down. I said sure. As she walked in the kitchen I noticed how her silk robe showed off her perfectly shaped ass at the end of her long, slender waistline. She came out of the kitchen, turned off the TV, and said, "Come in here." I followed her into her bedroom. It was just as clean as the rest of the house and her scent filled the air. As she sat my drink down, she told me to get comfortable. Then she asked if I wanted a hanger for my suit. We lay back on the pillows watching TV. Then she turned to me and threw her arm across my chest and put her thigh across mine. And we had one of the most sensual kisses I'd ever had. My penis got harder than the times in 1929. That's pretty hard. We must have kissed for two minutes. She said, "That was nice."

I said, "Yeah? Check this out." I stood at the end of the bed. While our eyes locked, I slid my boxers and T-shirt off. Then I crawled up over her real slow and poised, in a catlike fashion stalking his prey. She let out a pleasant little giggle. By this time I gave her a deep, sensual kiss and I went to work. As I nibbled gently on her earlobe and gently moved down her neck, her breathing started getting heavier. Then I ran my tongue down around her cleavage to her nipples as I gently caressed her breast. I went back and forth on her nipples to find out which one was the most sensitive. Like any good hunter, I study my prey to find out the best way to kill it. Sure enough, she gave me my weapon—the left one. As she let out a low, guttural sigh, I slowly worked my tongue down her stomach, nibbling lightly. Then her body started to flex as I got down to her pelvic area. She started to tremble. She said, "Oh, Tim, my body is tingling so hard." I could see she was getting very moist. I pulled her leg up slowly and ran my tongue down her inner thigh all the way to her toes. As I nibbled and sucked on her toes, she said, "Oh, Tim, where have you been all my life?" Then I worked my way up to my favorite place. It tasted so sweet. Her body twisted and then—splash—it was a river of love juice. I still didn't stop. As I licked and sucked on her clit, I found that spot on the inside right behind her clit and gently rubbed it. I paid special attention to her clit and her G spot for it seemed like five minutes. She came two more times. When I inserted my penis, she let out a piercing scream. Her body just started thrashing. I couldn't believe it; she was coming again. Then I pulled out and turned her over and did it doggy style. Then it started popping and spitting so hard my pelvic area was soaked. Her ass was so wet and round and firm, it felt like it even got harder. As I stroked it faster and faster she turned to me with tears in her eyes. She said, "Why are you doing me like this?" I just smiled at her. Now I'm sweating like a runaway slave. As I was about to reach my peak, I felt her vagina tighten up; then it felt like it was trembling with the rest of her body. Then—bam—we came together, panting like we had just run ten miles. I hadn't been that turned on in a while. I mean, there were sweat and come everywhere. We had to change the sheets before we could lie down. It was funny—when she got up to get the sheets, her knees buckled. I laughed. She said, "It's not funny."

We got the sheets changed and lay down. She gave me a kiss and then started kissing and rubbing my chest. I started getting another erection. I took her hand and put it on my penis. She said, "I can't believe you. You better go to sleep." We fell asleep in each other's arms and that's where we woke up Sunday afternoon.

After we got up, she fixed something to eat while I was in the shower. I was a little skeptical at first, because I was told not to eat everyone's cooking. I said, "What the hell. She seems safe enough." Besides, I'd been living a lot more dangerous then that.

I went home and got some clothes out to go to a meeting. I used to love to go to meetings because, whether I shared or not, I always heard something that would help me. You see, I remembered how messed up. It was just a couple of years before. They told me that if I didn't want to go back to that life, then this is what I have to do every day. So that's what I did. What NA has shown me is how to live without drugs and alcohol, which had been a part of my life for so long.

When I got to the meeting we did the normal—sat around and talked before the meeting. The meeting started with the Serenity Prayer: "God grant me the serenity to accept the things I cannot change; courage to change the things I can; and wisdom to know the difference." We do this before every meeting to usher in the Holy Spirit, so he might open our minds and give us peace. This is truly a spiritual program. If you listen and are open-minded, you'll always get what you need.

Today, one of the topics was relationships. This really got my attention. The guy had shared how he was married and had another woman on the outside. He ran like this for a long time. One night he was out on one of his runs, and when he came home his wife was in bed with someone else. He shared how that crushed him and that it took everything he had in him not to pick up drugs or alcohol—just to hold on until he could get to a meeting and dump it. That means, share it. They say, "Pain shared is pain lessened." Then it came time for feedback—this is where other members try to give hope, strength, and experience on your situation. Sometimes it works out, and sometimes it's a bashing session. That's why it's good to have a sponsor, so you can tell him or her things that you don't want other people to know but need to get off your chest so you can stay clean and sober.

It happened that there were some older members there that had been through similar stuff. They shared what they had gone through, why it happened, and how God brought them through. What I got out of it was that greed and self-centeredness are at the core of our disease. That's why we chase all those women—to make ourselves feel good. We don't consider the women and their feelings. When it turns around on us, then we get pain behind it and decide to change. Hmmmmmmmmm. This sounds familiar.

I left the meeting and called Mary to see how she was doing. I hadn't talked to her in a couple of days. She said she was fine. She asked me to come by, but I was too tired, especially after being with

Darla Saturday night. We talked for a minute; then I told her I would call her tomorrow and she said OK and we hung up.

Then I called Darla. She said, "Hi, Tim," like she was really glad to hear from me. She said, "I wondered if you were going to call."

I said, "You know I was." I told her, "I really enjoyed myself last night.She said she did too. "In fact," she said, "I'm still feeling last night." She said that when she answered the phone her stuff started throbbing again. She said it had been a while for her too. She had never in her life been done like that before. "Where did you learn that?"

I told her, "Here and there."

She said, "I don't know where you learned it, but I'm glad you did."

As time went on, I was starting to feel better and better. This was the first time since I had started getting high that I had been away from everything for a week, let alone a year.

I went home to see Donna and the kids one weekend. I had a real good visit. They really enjoyed me being there and I enjoyed being there also. While I was there Donna took a bath. When she came out she had on a terry cloth robe. She had on a little aqua teddy with just enough ass hanging out to give me a woody. Then she came and sat on my lap. She whispered in my ear, "You want some of this, don't you?" I said no. Then she rubbed my penis through my pants. She said, "I can't tell." Then she gave me a long, juicy kiss. I always loved the way she kissed. Then it happened—we went upstairs and did what we do.

I got up, cleaned up, and went and played with the children a little more. I hugged them and told them I loved them and left. I got back to Cincy. I stopped at a telephone and called Darla. I told her that I was just getting back from Dayton. She asked if I was coming by. I said, "Sure, I'll stop by for a minute." I got there and she greeted me with a big hug and a kiss. Man, I loved those lips. Her girls were in their beds and it wasn't long before we were in hers.

She said, "I want to show you something." She opened up her robe. She had on a fishnet body stocking; it was crotchless. I had never seen one of those before. This turned me on so much I pushed her back on the bed and gave her a good tongue lashing. Then she got on top and started riding me. This looked real freaky with this body stocking on. Then she grabbed me by the hand and pulled me in the kitchen. She sat me down in one of the kitchen chairs. Then she took the body stocking off and turned around and sat down on me. But this time she straddled me and put it in from behind. With her hands on my knees and feet on the floor, she started working it up and down and around and around until it started popping like the Fourth of July. Then I put my arms around to the front and gently pulled her lips open and started rubbing her clit. She got frantic then. She slammed her ass down on me like she was going to drive us right through the floor. She was rocking back and forth very violently. I had never felt a vagina this wet and hot before. I pushed her down on me harder with my forearms while I was still gently rubbing her clit. All of a sudden her body locked; then she started moving her ass like she was running a race. She said, "Baby, I'm coming again."

I said, "Hold it a little bit and we will do it together."

She said, "I can't...I can't...I can't.

I said, "Alright, I'm ready." She said OK while thrashing violently. Then it happened with a big gush. She just lay back on me and I held her right there sitting in her kitchen on the chair. Her body was so warm laid back against me. I loved it.

Then I went home. I took a shower and got ready for bed. I called Mary to see how she was doing. She asked if she could come by for a minute. I told her I had to get up in the morning to go to work. She said, "That's fine. I won't stay long." I told her to call when she was on her way so I could let her in the security door.

She called and I went down to let her in. I lived on the seventh floor. It must have taken a couple of minutes to get down there. When I got to the door she was pulling up. I let her in, gave her a hug, and turned towards the elevator. Then she grabbed my ass and said, "I've been missing that." We got on the elevator. As soon as the door closed, she unzipped my pants and in her mouth it went. I was so glad no one wanted to get on the elevator for two reasons: the embarrassment, and it was feeling so damn good, despite the fact that I had never done that before. Now, how could you let a woman like that go? I knew I had to, though, because my feelings for Darla were growing stronger. I thought, *I'll worry about that later.* You know, it's real hard to think with your penis in someone's mouth. She was good too. Let's just say that by the time we got to my floor, she shouldn't have been thirsty.

When we got to my apartment, my knees were a little weak so I sat on my bed—oh, by the way, this was an efficiency. That's why I got to the bed so quickly. She started taking my clothes off, asking me questions like, "Where have you been? What have you been doing? Why haven't you called?" I told her I was giving her a break as I was sitting there looking at her nakedness. I started getting another erection. She pushed me back on the bed and started pulling my pants off and said, "A break is not what I need. What I need is some of this dick."

Mary had a nice, thick, hard body—one that was hard to resist. I just lay back and let her do her thing. When she got finished, I flipped her over and started working on mine. It seemed like it was taking forever. I guess it gets like that when you have had sex three times in one day. So I turned her around so I could hit it from behind. Looking at a woman's ass vibrate when I hit it from behind turned me on for some reason. I guess it was the fact that I could feel it vibrating around my penis inside her. She started getting louder. Then she said, "Damn it, Tim, I'm coming again."

I said, "Are you mad or something?"

She said, "Hell no, baby." She said, "I want you to come with me." As the sensation got stronger, I hit it harder and harder. She got louder and louder.

Finally, her stuff started gripping my penis like it was pulsating. I said, "Here it comes, baby."

She said, "Give it to me." Then we fell on the bed like two deer shot by a hunter.

In the morning when I woke up, every muscle in my body was sore. I hadn't had sex three times in one day since before my addiction really took over. So I got my clothes together and took a shower to get ready for work. While I was cooking breakfast, I called my sponsor to see how he was doing, and I told him what went on. He quickly explained to me how sex could be another form of addiction, because as addicts we look for instant gratification; how having a lot of women just boosts our ego and gives us a false sense of pride. He said that I needed to take a look at that, because the same things that make me laugh can make me cry. You know what we do to hide from pain. We cover it up with drugs and alcohol. I told him thanks. I said, "I love you, man." I got off the phone, got dressed, and went to work.

I thought about what he said all day. When I got off work I went to a meeting. I put the topic out on the floor and told what I did. More than one person, male and female, told how they had gone through the same thing and when it all came down they ended up with no one. Even the one they really cared about left them, and it hurt them so bad that they went and got high over it.

So I really started thinking about it. In fact, it started to bother me. I really liked Darla, but Mary and Donna wouldn't leave me alone. Sure enough, Darla called me and she needed to see me. I went over to her house. She said, "Have a seat." This time seemed real different. She said, "Tim, are you fooling around?"

I asked her, "What makes you think that?"

She said, "I told you my body was very sensitive. I went to the doctor and I have an infection."

I said, "What kind?"

She said, "Chlamydia. So what have you been doing?" I had to fess up. I told her about Donna but not about Mary. She started crying and asked me, "How could you do me like that?" I told her I didn't plan to. I told her how Donna seduced me. She said, "What? You can't control your penis?" Then she said, "Let me help you. Get out."

I said, "Darla, please."

Crying even harder, she said again, "Get out." I can't remember the last time I felt so bad. It felt like someone stuck a knife right through my heart. Then out of nowhere, something said, "Go get a hit. It'll be alright."

I said, "Oh, hell, no." I stopped at the nearest phone and called my sponsor. I told him what had just happened.

I guess he heard the pain in my voice. He asked, "Where are you?" I told him. He said, "Get your ass over here right now. Tim, don't do anything stupid. Bring your ass over here right now."

So I got over to his house. He greeted me with a hug as we do in NA—the motto is, "Hugs, not drugs." While we hugged I broke down in tears. I mean, I was hurt. He got me some tissue and something to drink. Then he lit my ass up. He said, "What did I tell you about trying to run so many women? Man, that's what we did in our old life. When we get over here, it's about changing everything, including old behaviors. Old behavior is what kept us using drugs and alcohol. Later we went to a meeting." I just sat there and listened because I was really feeling some things and it didn't feel good. When I got home I called Darla. At first she didn't want to talk to me. Being the salesman I am, I broke her resistance down. I let her know how I felt about her. I apologized to her and told her that I loved her and hung up the phone.

I called Mary and told her that we needed to chill for a while. She asked why. I told her that I was going through some things and needed to clear my head. She said, "Come over here, and I'll clear it for you."

I said, "No, not tonight, but I will be in touch." Darla and I were never the same anymore. This was the spring of 1993. I had been clean about two and a half years now, and I still hadn't learned. I found out my sex addiction was as bad as my alcohol and drug addiction. I found out that drugs and alcohol were just a symptom of what was really wrong.

By this time I had started selling weed again, practicing old behaviors. After I got rid of Mary, two more took her place. It's not that I didn't love Darla, I was sick. Even though I wasn't using, I was still sick. What I was taught growing up was deeply embedded in me—what I know now as nonexistent virtues. So as in times before, I tried a geographical change, not realizing that no matter where I go, I am still there.

In about May 1993 I transferred to North Carolina. I moved back with my dad. So I check in at work and everything's good at work. Then one day, in walks this little cutie. She reminded me of Whitley on *A Different World*; she even had a cute little southern drawl. So here we go again. I'm talking to her about TVs at first. Then it started to get a little more personal. I found out a lot, like she was single, had a decent job, had her own house and a car, which was a plus—not to mention her thin frame, light brown eyes, and nice ass. So they delivered the TV. She called me and said they didn't hook it up right—could I come over and fix it. I said sure. I got off work, found her house, went in, and set her channels. She said, "Are you in a hurry?"

I said, "No, I don't have anywhere to be."

She said, "Do you want a drink?"

I said, "No, thank you," so we sat and talked. I thought about what was going on and tried to resist. It was hard but I did it. I was really trying to be good. It's good she worked third shift; that made it easier. So I left and stopped by Ms. Grace's house—this was my dad's girlfriend. Ms. Grace had two sons that were living with her at the time. Now one had this girlfriend that used to give him hell. I tried to tell him that she was trying to play him. She was fine too. She was one of those thick Gastonia chicks with hazel eyes.

She started picking at me one day. I told her she had better leave me alone. I told her I would take her to Kings Mountain and do something to her. She said, "You ain't going to do nothing. You are all talk."

I said, "You think so?" She said yeah. I said, "Alright, let's go." We got in the car and went to Kings Mountain. I played with her vagina all the way there—the whole twelve miles practically. When we got to the house, it was straight to the room. She took her clothes off. She had some of the nicest breasts I ever saw. Man, it was on.

We must have screwed for thirty to forty-five minutes straight—till she said, "I've had enough. You can't just be screwing me like this." She said, "Take me home." I said OK. I got up and took her home. I don't know what happened to her after that. I don't remember ever seeing or talking to her again.

The next day I went to work. Charlene called and said, "Thanks again for fixing my TV," and asked me if I wanted to have lunch. I said sure. We met at Shoney's. We sat and talked for about forty-five minutes. I was almost late getting back. She was so cute. The sun was shining through the bay windows, lighting up those pretty brown eyes. I was mesmerized. What made it even better is the fact that she was paying. She asked, "What are you going to do when you get off?"

I said, "Nothing, I guess."

She said, "Good. Stop by—I want to show you something."

I said, "I will see what I can do." I got off work and I called her to tell her I was on my way. I got there and she came to the door in her robe. She asked if I wanted some tea or something. I said sure. She got it and brought it to the living room and sat down beside me. We watched TV for a minute. Then I asked her, "What was it you wanted to show me?"

She said, "You want to see it now?"

I said, "I don't know. What is it?"

She smiled and turned her body, laid her back on the arm of the couch, propped her knees up, and opened her legs as wide as all outdoors. She said, "What do you think about that?"

I was speechless for about fifteen seconds it seemed. It's kind of hard to think when blood is rushing from your brain to your penis. I said, "Oh, that is so beautiful." It was, too. I said, "May I kiss it?"

She said, "Please do." She had the sweetest scent and her skin was as soft as cotton. As I licked it and worked around the clit, it seemed like her pussy started gasping for air. I mean, it was opening and closing on its own. Then I stuck my finger in and found the G spot. It was so wet and wide open I put another finger in it. Soon I had three fingers in it. I was working my hand slowly back and forth, being sure to keep pressure on her G spot and my lips gently around her clit, flicking it lightly with my tongue. She said, "I knew you were a freak." Then she screamed. Her body flexed so hard, I thought it was going to snap. Then her ass slammed back down on the couch. Her whole body went into convulsions. There was cum everywhere. She was on fire. She said, "Tim, please fuck me. I need you; it's been so long." I picked her up and carried her to the bedroom. I took my clothes off and climbed up on top of her and put it in. Instantly, she started jumping and bucking wildly. I came with her—it took about thirty seconds. She said, "Hell, no! You are not getting away that easy." She started sucking my penis; she was real good. I don't know what she did, but it came back up as fast as it went down. Then she turned around, put her head and shoulders and breast on the bed, and pointed her ass to the moon. When I put my penis in it, it was so wet and hot. It felt like a bowl of warm Jell-O. Instantly it started spitting and popping. She said, "Damn! I am coming again. Shit, Tim, you got some good dick."

I said, "You like it?"

She said, "Oh, baby, I love it." I must have ridden it just like that for about fifteen minutes. She said, "Baby, come on. I can't come anymore. You have to hurry up. Come on. Give it to me."

I said, "You can't come anymore, huh?"

She said, "Baby, I'm done."

I said, "Bet, watch this." I put it in as deep as I could. I held it there and reached around and played with her clit. Then I worked it in and out. I felt it getting wetter. When I got to the top, I kept rubbing her clit and gently working the head in and out just enough to hit that spot.

She said, "Oh, no, I can't take it." It started spitting and popping and gripping like there was no tomorrow. Then we came together. I put it deep inside her so she could feel it coming. She said, "Oooh." Her voice was trembling like someone poured a bucket of ice in her ass. I got up, washed myself up, and went home. She had to go to work.

When I got home my dad told me that Ann had called me. I said, "Ann who?" He told me it was the daughter of the woman he used to see. He told me what she looked like. I couldn't trust my dad's judgment, so I called her. I had to get to work the next day, so I told her that I would get with her when I got off work.

I went to work the next day. Things were going good. I made a few sales and I was trying not to call Charlene, but that's all that was on my mind. At about one o'clock I called her. She was still asleep. I left her a message on her machine. After an hour or so she called back. She said, "I'm not messing with you anymore; you don't play fair."

I said, "Why did you call then?" She said she was being polite by returning my call. I said, "Thanks."

She said, "You are something else." I told her that I had customers coming in and I had to go. I would call her later.

I was about to get off work and I gave Charlene a call. I told her that I was thinking about her and just wanted to say hello before I left. She had to go to work, so I was going to let her rest. I stopped by the house and called Darla in Cincy to see how she was doing. She said she was doing OK. She said, "Tim, you know, I'm seeing someone."

I said, "I figured that. Do you like him?"

She said, "He is OK."

I said, "As long as he treats you OK. I don't want to have to come up there and put a bullet in his head." I said, "You know, I still love you."

She said, "Yeah, right. I'll talk to you later, Tim." I said bye in a sorrowful tone.

I called Ann. She told me to come and get her. I needed something to make me feel better since I wasn't getting high. I guess this was it. I went to Shelby to get her. I had to sneak her out because she was seeing someone. It didn't seem right, but I needed a fix, so what the hell. She came out of the house. She was dark and lovely—nice body, but for some reason I wasn't really feeling it. I took her back to Kings Mountain anyway. We talked on the way about a lot of nothing. I was not feeling this at all. She didn't even have anything to offer except a piece of ass, plus I had to sneak. We got to Kings Mountain and had sex, but it was not the normal Timmy show—just the basic OK let's do this and get you the hell back home. After I dropped her off, I thought about it all the way home. *Why am I doing this shit? I really have a problem. Just like I would go to any lengths for my drugs, I'm doing the same thing with sex. I guess it is true what they say. Addiction affects all areas of our life.* I was using sex to take the place of drugs. This wasn't good.

The next day I found a meeting to go to. I realized that using drugs was just a symptom of the disease of addiction. Anything that makes me feel good, I would chase it. When it stopped working, it could lead me back to my drug of choice. I found a meeting and the message was basically the same: how to live life after drugs and how the solution to our problem was spiritual. We talked about a higher power. They used this term so as not to offend anyone. We were told to find a God of our own understanding. I didn't have a problem with that, because I have always believed in Jesus—even though most times you couldn't tell. I knew for a fact that it was God's grace and mercy that were protecting me and keeping me from harm. They also said that I should turn my will over to him. That is where the problem was. I would turn it over but take it right back.

That gave me something to think about. I was really going to put my all into it. I got home around ten or so; then the phone rang. It was Charlene. She asked where I had been. I told her to a meeting. She said she just wanted to say hi before she went to work. She asked if I had to go to meetings every day. I said, "I need to."

She said, "You aren't drinking or getting high, are you?"

I said, "No, but there are other issues that I am dealing with."

She said, "I guess I just don't understand."

I said, "You'll be alright."

She said, "Well, I have to go now."

I said, "Have a good night."

She said, "Tim…" Then it got quiet like she wanted to say something. Then she said, "Never mind. I'll talk to you tomorrow." We got off the phone.

I was getting in the shower when the phone rang again. It was Darla. I said, "Hey, girl, what's up?"

She said, "Nothing. I was just thinking about you."

I asked, "Where is your new friend?"

She said, "I don't know." Then she said, "Tim, he can not fuck."

I said, "What is wrong?"

She said, "He doesn't know how to do anything."

I said, "Well, baby, I am a tough act to follow."

She said, "Tim, I really miss you. I need you here." I told her I was off Sunday; maybe I would take off Saturday and come that way. She said, "If you do, I will get a hotel so we don't have to worry about him popping up."

I said, "You don't have to worry about that anyway, do you?"

She said, "Ha ha. Very funny."

I said, "I will call you Wednesday and let you know what's up."

She said, "Please come, Tim. I need you."

I went to work the next day and told them I needed Saturday off. I told them I was going to Ohio. They thought I was going to see my children. I told Charlene I was going and she got a little upset. That's when I saw her little mean streak. I mean, she had a real attitude. I said, "I have to see my children."

She said, "Right. You are going to see that bitch." I know now that was addictive behavior—lying to get what I wanted.

Thursday I got off a little early. I called Charlene and I told her I was coming over. She said, "Whatever." She still had an attitude. I got over there. She came to the door in some daisy dukes and a cutoff top. I sat down on the couch. She came and stood in front of me and said, "I don't want you to go." I told her I had not seen my children in a while and I was going anyway. She said, "You are going to leave this good stuff all alone?" I pulled her on my lap; she was straddling me. I started kissing her and I told her that she wasn't going to need anything while I was gone. I was going to take care of her right now, and she was right—she was good. We made love so long she could not go to work. In fact, she slept until midnight. When we woke up, she said, "If you are going to see that bitch, you aren't going to have anything left. I am taking all your juice." Then she started in on me. I don't know where she got her skills, but this girl was bad.

When I went to work on Friday, I had my clothes in the car. I left right from work. I drove all night. I was tired as hell after being with Charlene, getting up for work, then driving all night. If this wasn't addictive behavior, I don't know what is. I was truly putting my life in danger. I could have fallen asleep and ran off the mountain or something. If it wasn't for the six cups of coffee, I might have.

When I got to Cincy, I called her at work. She told me to go to the Red Roof Inn. I went and checked in. I was so amped from the coffee, I just lay in the bed and stared at the ceiling for I do not know how long. It reminded me of when I had smoked so much dope, I would lie there trying to get to sleep. When she got off work she came straight to the hotel. When I let her in, she jumped straight in my arms and wrapped her legs around me. The force knocked me back on the bed. We must have kissed for five minutes; man, I missed those big, juicy lips. We lay there and talked for a minute. She said she wanted to take a shower. I said, "Cool. I'll take one with you." We got in the shower and lathered up. She turned around so I could wash her back. She had the most perfectly shaped ass; it was firm too. It almost looked like if you would thump it, it would sound like one of those nice, crisp apples, but it was as soft as cotton. I pulled her to me. She turned her head and started kissing me as I rubbed her breast. This felt so good with the water running down our faces as I kept rubbing her nipples and breast. Her ass was pressed up against my pelvis. I got hard instantly. I slid my right hand down her long, slender body. I gently stroked her bush until I found her clit. When I rubbed it her knees buckled. She leaned forward with her hands on the wall. She said, "There it is, daddy. Get it." That water looked so good running down her back and the crack of her ass. It was almost as good as the act itself. I slid inside her; it was hot and wet.

I said, "You really missed me, didn't you?"

She said as she was panting, "You know I did." Then she started forcing herself against me harder and harder. Then came the explosion. We finished washing and got out of the shower. Then we got in the bed. She grabbed my penis and put it in her mouth and went to work. With her mouth on my penis, she moved into the 69 position. I said OK. I knew what she wanted, and I wanted to give it to her. So I grabbed her ass and spread her cheeks and did a little work of my own. Her body started trembling; then she came so hard some splashed in my face. Then I turned her over and rode that ass like a rhinestone cowboy. We must have made love for a solid hour.

When we were done, we held each other. She had tears in her eyes. She said, "Why did you have to go?" I told her I didn't want to hurt her anymore because I really did love her. But I was sick. I couldn't promise her that I would be faithful, because now that I was not getting high I was still dealing with the way I was raised. Then we both started crying and holding each other. Before I knew it, we were at it again.

We went and got something to eat at Friday's. While we were talking, I apologized again for giving her that infection. She said she understood how that could happen. She said Donna and I will probably always have a connection because of the children. I said, "Yes, but I hate how she made me weak." I said, "You know how I feel about you. I don't need anyone else, just like I don't need to be around dope. I don't need to be around her either." We got finished eating.

She went home and I went to a meeting. I saw my old sponsor. He asked me if I was going to see my children. I said I had to get back to North Carolina so I could go to work. He said, "You drove five hundred miles for some sex. Man, you are sick. You really need to take a look at that."

So the next morning I called Darla up and told her goodbye and left. I had plenty of rest. My mind was clear and the five-hundred-mile trip gave me plenty of time to think. Mostly, all I could think of was how good it was to be with Darla again and that good stuff. In fact, my penis must have gotten hard forty times between there and home. It reminded me of when I was trying to get clean. They said to rewind the whole tape so I could remember the pain it caused me.

I got home and called Charlene and told her I was home. Then I called Darla and told her I made it back. She said, "You got back quick." I told her that I was thinking of her all the way. Then she said, "My friend is here. I've got to go." That really hurt, hearing that—like I expected her to just stop seeing him. She did a little later, though. I went back to work. My coworkers asked about the trip and how my children were. I had to lie. I couldn't tell them I just went to get some sex. Not only would it sound stupid, but they would know that I had lied in the first place.

Later in the week I had gone over to Charlene's. We were in the bed getting it on. Suddenly the hall light came on and the bedroom door came open. Her baby's daddy had come in through the kitchen window. At first it scared me. Then he went in his son's room and got him up and said, "Look at your mother. She's fucking another man." As if he didn't know anyway.

I thought, *This must be the stupidest motherfucker in the world.* I could have blown his brains out. Charlene grabbed her robe and ran around the corner to her sister's house and called the police. Then he looked at me and left. I went home. I said, "This shit is too crazy for me." I thought about it on the way home. I said, "Shit, he could have killed me. Hell, she could be trying to play him too. What else would make him take a chance like that?" I said, "Shit, this is some good sex, but it's not that damn good to put my life on the line."

This was late 1993. Shortly after that, I was transferred back to Cincy. It was a trip. The two managers were arguing about which store I was going to. I ended up at the Ridge Avenue store. I started staying with some friends of mine. By this time, I guess I had stayed away too long. Darla had gotten over me, but she let me know that if I got a divorce, it was on. I wasn't ready to do that, and besides, Donna and I were starting to be civil towards each other. I just didn't know where that was going.

It was real hard totally letting go. I have to admit I still cared for her. After all, she is the mother of my children. I later found out that was part of my addictive behavior also—always returning to something familiar when things got tough.

I started at the Ridge store. As always, things were getting pretty good. I had also gotten back in touch with El so I could get back to selling weed. Since we lived in the ghetto, that wasn't a bad idea either. I would serve a few hookers and some personal friends.

I had talked to my brother. He informed me that Spunky's was closing and they were having a party this weekend. So a friend and I rode up. I called Donna to see if she wanted to go. She said sure. We went to the party. I mean, everyone was there. It was like a family reunion—dignitaries, my barber, just everyone. I mean, the party was jumping. I slipped away from Donna. As I was walking to the other side of the club, there stood this six-foot-tall goddess. As we looked eye-to-eye, I smiled and introduced myself. She said, "Hi.

My name is Tara." She had a pretty smile and a twinkle in her eyes. We talked for a few seconds. I gave her my business card and told her to call me. I went back to the other side where Donna was and got her and we danced for a while. We had a good time. I felt kind of bad about what I had done, but what the hell, I had already done it. I never went out with Donna meaning to pick up other women. Sometimes things happen. After we left the club, I went back to Donna's and stayed the night. You can imagine what happened then. The next morning my roommate and I left. I came back to Cincy. I dropped him off at home and went to work. Later that day, Tara called. I told her that I didn't expect her to call so soon. She said that she didn't have anything to do, so she called. I asked what she had planned for the evening. She said she didn't have any plans. So I invited her down. She said sure. So I gave her directions to the store. I figured out how long it would take her to get from Dayton to the store. I said to myself, *She probably won't be about anything—just another pretty girl looking for a free ride.*

I was standing at the front of the store about the time I thought she would be pulling in. All of a sudden, I saw a black BMW pull into the parking lot. I couldn't tell if it was her for sure. Then the car pulled into the parking spot. As I watched, she got out. I said, "Oh, snap, it is her." Then I got insecure. I thought, *What would she want with someone like me?* As I look back on it, I guess I had a low-self-esteem attack. Then I put my game face on. I said, "Oh, that's right. I am the man." I watched her as she walked toward me with long, sexy strides. The closer she got, the better she looked. Mind you, I met her in a dark club, which tends to hide imperfections. Plus I didn't have a lot of time to stand around and check her out.

I opened the door for her and she came in. I gave her a hug and thanked her for coming. A feeling came over me like I had taken a super-sized hit. I got anxious, my palms got sweaty, and I was nervous as hell, but I shook it off and told her I had to go clock out. I went and clocked out, came back through, and hollered at my cats. I told James to come up front and meet my girl. Then we left. I had her follow me to the apartment. We went in so I could change. I introduced her to my roommate and got in the shower. I was kind of embarrassed. Our apartment was not the nicest, but it was clean. It was also on the hoe stroll. Looking at the way she was dressed, and what she was driving, she had class written all over her. I knew she came from somewhere better than this, so I didn't know how she felt about it. I came out of the shower and put a towel around me, and I came into the living room and told her to be thinking about what she wanted to eat. I could tell by the expression on her face that she liked what she saw. I put on my best cologne. Then I put on the sharpest suit I had. When I came out everybody was like, damn. I have to admit I was kind of fresh. As you could tell by the first part of the book, I am no stranger to dressing. So I took her by the hand and helped her up off the couch. She said, "Um um um."

I asked her, "What's wrong?"

She said, "Not a thing."

I said, "So what do you want to eat?"

She said, "This is your town. You pick." When we got outside, she said we could take her car. She asked if I would drive because she was tired. I unlocked her door first and opened it for her. After she sat down, I closed the door and walked around the back of the car as I often did to see if she would unlock the door. I heard the locks click to unlock my door. That showed me she was thinking about me. So I came to the conclusion that she wasn't selfish.

As I sat in the car, I noticed the smell. It wasn't brand-new, but it still had a little of the new-car smell. The leather felt so good. This was my first time in a BMW this new. I asked her what year it was. She told me it was a 1990. I had already seen it was a 325i. I asked her which one of her men bought it for her. She got a lightweight attitude and told me she bought it herself. I said, "OK, I apologize." I said to myself, *Bingo.* Then I headed toward I-75. I asked her if she smoked weed.

She said, "Yes, do you have some?" Then I pulled an ounce out of my pocket. She said, "Damn, you always roll like that?"

I said, "Pretty much." I always kept it like that, because whenever I sold some, I would just take whatever they wanted out of the bag. Because if I would get caught with it, as long as it's in one bag, they couldn't get me for trafficking. I gave her the bag and told her to roll herself a joint.

As she started rolling, she said, "Man this stuff is sticky." I asked if she liked seafood. She said sure, so I headed for the waterfront. She got the joint rolled and lit it. After she finished coughing, she passed it to me.

I said, "I don't smoke."

She said, "Well, what are you doing with it?"

I told her, "Now you are asking too many questions."

Then she said, "I should have known."

I said, "Known what?"

She said, "I saw you at the club kickin' it with the fellas. I thought that you all were just old friends. You told me you had a job and you lived in Cincy, but you are just a thug in a suit."

I said, "Baby, I ain't no thug. I just got a few thuggish ways."

She said, "Who was that girl you were with?" I was like, damn, you don't miss a thing, do you? She said, "I told you I was checking you out." I told her what was up and she asked if we were going to work it out. I said I didn't know. Then she said, "You should." I said to myself I was about to work something else out right now. We went to T.G.I. Friday's. She said she had never been to the waterfront before. I told her to stick around and she would get to do a lot of things she had never done before. She said, "Like what?"

I said, "You'll see, baby." So we ate. Then we left and went to Skipper's. It was so crowded that we couldn't get a table, so we sat at the bar. We ordered some drinks. She said, "You don't drink either?"

I said, "No, I don't." Then I told her my story—about what I had been through and how God had spared my life. How I was a member of NA. We sat and talked for the longest time.

Then she said, "I want to dance. You do dance, don't you?"

I said, "Very funny. Come on." We were out there for the longest time. Then they played a slow song and I pulled her to me.

She said, "Damn, you smell good." All I was thinking about was those super-sized breasts pressed against me. Yes, she was very blessed. It was about time for the club to close. We were sitting there talking and I was holding her hand.

I looked deep into her eyes and said, "Tara, do you want to make love to me?" She said yes so we left Skipper's and went to the Armada Inn.

We got in the room, we started kissing, then the clothes came off. I had no idea her breasts were that big. She had the biggest breasts of any woman I had ever been with. The sex was decent—not the best I had ever had, but certainly not the worst. It was kind of fun playing with her breasts; she seemed to really enjoy it. The next morning she took me home. We kissed goodbye. This was the beginning of a different kind of a relationship, because she was daddy's little girl and very spoiled. As time went on, this would be the thing that turned me off the most. It was also one of the busiest sexual times in my life since I had stopped selling cocaine.

I started hanging out at a club called Sonny's with a guy I worked with. His girl was a waitress there. She had a friend named Rene. She was cute and had a bangin' body. I mean, it was just right. Plus she was bowlegged. That really turned me on. She was originally from Jersey, so she had an accent. We ended up getting closer. When it came to sex, she couldn't get enough—doggy style, missionary, riding, 69, whatever, it didn't matter. I was impressed. Whenever I went to see her, I needed a full night's rest. She didn't have much but she was trying.

Soon I quit Circuit City and went to work at Swallen's, which proved to be a mistake, because they soon went out of business. In the meantime, this is where I met Sherry. She was probably the finest—well, one of the finest women I had ever been with. She was a little boyish though, which was OK. She had a hustling spirit like me. One thing she had messed up was she thought she was going to work me. She bought me a pound of weed and thought I was going to give her the money. I had gone and spent the night at Donna's, and she got upset. She didn't want anything else to do with me, which was cool because I could already see that we were not going to get along.

It was 1994. I moved back to Dayton. I was back in the house with my children and I was loving it. They had gotten older now. I looked at what God had created through me and I realized how blessed I was. I still couldn't shake the old behavior. The devil still had a hold on me, but I couldn't see it. I still thought it was OK to be married and still have other women and sell drugs. I started working at Sam's Club. I was doing outside sales. This was cool. I got to run all over Ohio and get paid for it. I was working with a girl named Betty. She was a white girl with a big butt. I found that kind of sexy. Plus she was from a town called Yellow Springs. I had heard some freaky stories about Yellow Springs. This made me even more interested. We became friends. We would talk all the time. I kept her laughing. She told me she was married to a black guy. That didn't surprise me, because she had the kind of ass only a brother could appreciate. She caught me looking at it once. She asked if I liked big butts. I said, "You know it."

She said, "My husband has a cousin with a big butt. I'll introduce you to her." She called her from the phone room at work. Her name was Sharon. She was from Yellow Springs also. So I talked to her and set up a meeting.

I met her at the Dayton Street Gulch, which was a bar in Yellow Springs. I got there early, sat down, and had a drink—my usual cranberry and orange juice. I asked the bartender if he knew Sharon.

He said he didn't. I could tell he was lying. A few minutes later a black girl walked in. The bartender whispered something in her ear and then looked at me. I said to myself, *This must be her.* She came over. I said, "Sharon?"

She said, "Timothy?"

I said, "Yes. Good to meet you."

She said, "Same here." She had a real cool demeanor—kind of nonchalant, which was OK. She moved with a slow, steady stroll, strong and secure. This kind of turned me on. We sat there and talked. I bought her a drink and I got my usual. She noticed I didn't drink. She said to me, "You don't drink?" I told her I had not drunk in a few years. Then I told her my story and what I had been through. She was impressed. We sat and had a couple more drinks. Then I walked her to her car and left.

I went back to work the next day and I thanked Betty for introducing us. Sharon was completely different from any of the others. She was only five foot three and kind of thick. But she had a cuteness about her. A couple of days later I went to her house. She had a cute little one-bedroom apartment. It was clean though. That was one of the things I looked for—how a woman kept her house. We were sitting and talking. I asked her if she smoked weed. She said, "Sure. Do you have some?"

I said, "Sure," and I pulled out a bag of weed and rolled a joint.

She said, "How do you know you can smoke weed in my house?"

I said, "Oh, you told me that you smoked."

She said, "Oh." Then she said, "I thought you didn't get high."

I said, "I don't. This is for you."

She said, "OK. Thanks." I asked her if she knew anyone that wanted to buy some. She said she would make some calls for me. This turned out to be a pretty profitable relationship. I stayed with her half the night, made a few sales, and went home. It was about a thirty-minute ride from Yellow Springs to Dayton. That's one thing—I always tried to keep my girls spread out, mostly out of Dayton, so I wouldn't get caught.

It was now 1995. I made a sales call at Fairborn Buick. This was another turn in my life. I was giving the manager my sales pitch and he ended up selling me. He asked me if I had ever thought about selling cars. I told him I never wanted to be a car salesman, because of the shady image they had. Go figure. He said he understood. He assured me that they didn't do business like that. I asked him how much I could expect to make. He said if I didn't make thirty-five to forty-five thousand my first year, I should find something else to do. Knowing that I had always excelled at any sales job I had, and the fact that I was only making about eighteen thousand a year now, I said, "What the hell. I'll give it a shot."

I finished my day at Sam's and went over to Sharon's. This was the day it happened, and man, was it good. She was thirty-two and had never had any children. You can imagine the tight fit. On top of that, she had a real slow grind while she would flex her muscles. I had never come so quick in my life. It wasn't long before I was hard again; this time I put on a clinic. She said, "Damn, Timothy, what are you trying to do—choke me?" I guess I was going a little deep. She was different. She wasn't as passionate as most of the women I had been with, but she got wetter and wetter. When she came, she arched her back so hard she almost threw me off of her. When we finished, I made a couple of sales and went over to Tara's. I talked to her mom. They wanted me to pick her up at the airport. She was coming in from LA.

It was a nice, warm night—a great night for a ride—so it wasn't a bad trip at all. When she came out to the car, she gave me the biggest hug and kiss we had ever had. I thought she was going to do me right there. I put her bags in the car and she told me she had something for me. I asked her what it was. She said she would show me when we got back to the house. I said, "Cool." Then I gave her a joint I had ready for her. We got to the house and got the car unpacked.

She pulled out a bag and said, "Here." This was the funkiest warm-up suit I had ever seen. It was a turquoise green silk Nike warm-up suit with some Nike shoes. I had never seen a warm-up like that. She wouldn't let me know what it cost. Later, Los, one of the barbers at Creative Cut, told me he had seen it in a book for $250. I went and sat in with her mom and talked to her while Tara took a shower. Tara came out of the room at about twelve thirty or one o'clock. She said, "Let's go out back." They had a big yard with an in-ground pool. I sat on the end of the diving board while she smoked the rest of her joint. Then she said, "I have something else for you." She pushed me back on the diving board and proceeded to unzip my pants. Before I knew it, she was on her knees and my penis was in her mouth. I was like, damn, did you miss me? You have only been gone a week. She said, "Seems like you missed me too." Then she pulled up her sundress and straddled me right on the diving board. She had such long legs it was easy for her.

As she continued to ride up and down, her breathing started getting heavier. I said, "You better be quiet. Someone is going to hear us." She said so. There were bushes surrounding the yard like a privacy wall, so no one could see us. Her body started to shiver and her vagina started gripping and popping. All of a sudden I felt this warm flow all over me. She started grinding faster and faster. Then I came with her and she collapsed in my arms and kissed me and told me that she loved me.

I said, "I love you too." At least I thought I did. Actually, I don't know what it was. I knew I felt a certain way about her, but I felt that way about all the women. Why did I have this need for all these women? Was it my greed and self-centeredness? Hmmm. That's what had me so messed up on drugs and alcohol. As time went on, I found myself running like a chicken with his head cut off. I had Rene in Cincy, Sharon in Yellow Springs, Tara in Centerville, and of course Donna. It wasn't long before I forgot all about the program. Sex and money had taken the place of my recovery. I was sliding downhill. I was just too blind to see it.

Then it happened. It was 1996, a nice spring day. I was at the barber shop—you know, Creative Cut. I used to go there and sit for hours. It was more than just a place to get a haircut. We were like family. Not only did I have a relationship with the barbers, I watched a lot of boys grow into men. It was amazing to see God at work. I saw drug dealers get saved. I also saw the least likely go to prison or get killed. It made me really grateful. They were teasing me. They used to always ask me, "Which way are you going today? 75 south or 35 east or west?" because that's the way I rolled. G-man would always ask, "Which one of those lemons are you going to see today?" He would call my girls lemons because most of them were light-complexioned. So I got finished with my haircut, gave every-body dap, and rolled out.

I got in my car, pulled the visor down, and opened the mirror. I opened the sunroof, so the sun could beat down on my wavy locks. I said, "Damn, I look good." And I was feeling even better. I said, "Shit, it's been almost three years since I smoked a joint." Life was good and it was a beautiful, sunny day. Why not? *Let's smoke a joint, Tim,* I said to myself.

I sat there and rolled a joint while Prince was bangin' in my stereo. That's right—Prince. I had a couple thousand watts in my trunk; that made him sound even better.

I took off, fired up the joint, and hit 75 south on my way to Cincy to see Rene. By the time I got to the Centerville exit, I had smoked the whole joint, my dumb ass. I got high and paranoid. The bass was hitting upside my head so hard, I had to turn my music down. Finally, I had to turn it off. The bass was still hitting me too strong. I don't know how I made it to Cincy. At that point, I still had about forty miles to go. But I pulled it together somehow and made it.

When I got to Rene's, I gave her the rest of the weed I had taken out for myself. I told her what happened. She said, "Stupid," and then she laughed and we made love for about an hour an a half. I left and came home and sat around with the children for a while.

Things were really good, but I couldn't see how they were slowly slipping away. I had no NA in my life. I had totally gotten away from God. I was caught up again. I might as well have been smok-ing crack, because I was still out of control and getting deeper—as you will soon see.

One of my friends came over to my house. We were sitting around talking. He asked me if I wanted to go to a party with him. I said, "Sure." Maybe I could do a little business.

We went to the party and immediately my attention focused on the girl that was giving the party. I was such a whore. Anyway, her name was Darla. This turned out to be Darla #2. Even though she was nothing like Darla #1, she was good too. It's kind of like getting high. You are always chasing that first hit, but you can never seem to find it. So before we left, I got her number. She told me she was looking for a car. After a few days, I called her and she came out to the lot and bought one. We ended up having sex in the office.

Then I met V. I told her I was married. It really didn't matter to her. I just wanted to hit it. She was fine as hell. She was tall, slim, chocolate brown. She had an ass like a hooker and legs like a stripper. She had the kind of eyes you could get lost in. I told her if she found someone that she wanted to be with to let me know and I would get out of the way. We had kicked it for a while now. Man, she had the best head in the world. One time she went down on me, after about forty-five seconds it was a wrap. To this day, I haven't found anything that can compare. One day she had asked me to front her some weed so I did. When I went to get my money, she acted like she had an attitude. I didn't give a shit; I wanted her to give me my money. So one day she called me and told me she had found someone. I asked her if she liked him and if he treated her OK. She said yes. I said, "OK, baby, stay in touch." So after a couple of days, she called and said she was pissed at me. She said I acted like it didn't mean anything to me. I asked her, "What did you want me to do—cry and beg you to stay? I told you what the deal was, so don't be mad at me. I hope we can still be friends," and we hung up.

At this time things were really getting crazy sexually. Tara, Darla, Sharon, and Rene were starting to expect more out of me than I was prepared to give. Tara made me have sex with her one night.

I had gone over to her house one day just to chill. When I got ready to leave, she said, "Tim, I want some." I told her I was tired and wasn't really feeling it. She started getting demanding. She followed me to the car and sat in the passenger seat and wouldn't get out. She said, "Oh, yeah, you are going to give me some before you leave." So I walked up to her and put my penis in her mouth, and she did what she does. Then she got up and I sat down. Then she climbed on top of me and put my penis inside her. She was as hot as fire.

I said, "Damn, girl, what's wrong with you?"

She said, "I miss you. I need you, Tim."

I said, "You got me, baby." I made a couple of deep, hard thrusts. This started the flow. Then I slowed it up a little—long and steady strokes while I was smacking her ass.

She said, "Oh shit, Tim." Then she had back-to-back orgasms. As I speeded up just a little, we came together on the second one. Then she lay down on me with her body twitching. She said, "Tim, you are the best."

One weekend I told Donna I was going to a fish fry that my boss was giving. Instead, I went to Springfield to hang out with Sharon. I used to do that a lot. If it was any one of my women that you could say had me sprung, it would have been her. She wasn't the cutest of them all, but the sex was all that.

So, anyway, the plan was just to hang out, have some fun, have some sex, and go home. It just didn't turn out like that. By the time we got to the room I was so tired, I lay back on the bed and passed out. When I woke up, the birds were chirping, the sun was up, bright as hell, and my pager was blowing up. I mean, there was an APB out on me. Everyone was looking for me, from my wife to my sister. Since I didn't come home, they didn't know what happened to me. When I left, I was supposed to be coming home. When I didn't they got worried. My sister knew what I was into as well as my wife, so as far as they were concerned, anything could have happened.

When I got home, I told my wife I fell asleep over at one of my cats' houses—which she knew when I am dead tired that would be highly possible.

I had so much pressure on me. Between Donna and the children and all these women, I started drinking.

Then I started working at Mel Farr Linc-Merc. That's when I started slipping. Donna had an idea I was messing around but she never could prove it. When I came home I always had extra money, so that would pacify her.

One weekend I told her I was going on a run with one of my cats and I went to Springfield to spend the weekend with Sharon. Her grandmother belongs to an organization and they were having a ball, so we went to it. After that we went to the hotel. I couldn't wait to get into those draws. She had on a black dress that made those thick curves look so good. When we got to the room she didn't have enough time to get her dress off before I had my tongue in her vagina. She was saying, "No, Tim, you are going to make me come. No, baby, I don't want to...to...to...Oh, shit, Timothy. Oh, shit,

I'm coming." I didn't care. I kept on licking and sucking and sucking and licking. This is the first time I heard her scream. She always had quiet orgasms. She said, "Please, Timothy, I can't take it anymore." She tried to get up and I grabbed her by her arms and held her there. Then I buried my face and tongue as deep as I could. All of a sudden her body got as stiff as a board. Then she started shuddering. I got up and she balled up in a knot, still shuddering. I pulled my pants off, opened her legs, and crawled inside her. She said, "Damn you, Timothy. I can't take it." She started shuddering violently, saying, "Shit, shit, shit." This time I came with her and all of a sudden we were lying in a puddle of love.

About Tuesday my brother called. I was in the bathroom taking a dump and the phone was ringing. I came out and picked it up and we talked for about ten minutes. I told him all about my weekend. I didn't know the answering machine had picked up. I went to the barber shop. After I got my haircut I got a page from home. I was on my way there, so I didn't bother calling. When I got there, Donna was folding clothes in the bedroom. She said, "Tim, do you love me?"

I said, "Sure, baby."

She said, "How much?"

I said, "I love you more than anything in the world."

She said, "So how in the fuck could you do this to me then?" Then she played the answering machine. It had recorded my whole conversation with my brother. This time my salesman shit didn't work. She hit me in the jaw. It stunned me for a little while. All I could do was sit on the bed. I was wrong and all my shit was catching up with me.

After all that, it still didn't stop me. I met someone else the next week. If that's not the sign of an addict, I don't know what is. In spite of impending doom, I was going on to the bitter end.

It was about June 1996. It was a nice, sunny day. I had taken my car down on Salem to the car wash. A lady pulled up driving a new Aurora. You know I saw dollar signs. I watched her get out of her car. She was light-skinned, about five foot eight inches tall, kind of slim, in some nice jeans. I knew she was a freak because she had on a red wig.

I was putting a plan together to get her attention. I wanted her to come to me, so I was standing there looking at the temp tag in her rear window. The plan started unfolding. She came out and said, "Can I help you? Do you like what the hell you are looking at?"

I said, "Oh, I was just seeing what kind of tag that was."

I asked if she was from Michigan and she said, "No, but the car is."

Then I introduced myself. I said, "My name is Tim."

She said, "I'm D."

I shook her hand and said, "Nice to meet you." She had a firm handshake. We talked for a minute. I got a couple of laughs out of her. Then I asked if I could call her sometime. She said sure and she gave me her number and I gave her my card and put my cell number on it. I love it when a plan comes together.

After a couple of days I called her. I would have called sooner, but I was taking care of other things plus trying to keep things cool at home. I left a message on her machine. I told her I really enjoyed meeting her and had hopes of seeing her again. She called me back at work. I asked her what she had planned for the evening. She said she didn't have anything planned. I told her me and some of the guys were going to have some drinks and shoot some pool after work. I asked her if she wanted to go. She said sure.

She lived in back of the dealership. I picked her up and we went to the club. We really had fun. She was so classy. I liked her a lot. I took her home and we sat and smoked some weed. Then I left. I met up with the guys at Key West, which was a strip club. We went there a lot. This night I didn't sit at the stage. I was getting tired of watching my money walk away. I was at the pool table shooting pool. Then one of the dancers, named Rey Rey, came offstage and came over to shoot pool with me. She was a sexy little chocolate thing. We talked for a minute. I asked her if some of the girls wanted to buy some weed. She asked if I had some on me. I said, "Sure, let them check this out." I gave her a bud for show and she brought back one hundred dollars. I said, "Hmm, this could be good."

The next day all I could think about was D. Then she just happened to drop by on her way home. She looked good. She had on a suit like she just came from the office. She was looking very professional. She had some of the sexiest legs I had ever seen. I used to say she had Cincy legs because a lot of the girls from Cincy had some nice legs. She asked me to stop by when I got off. I said, "I'll see what I can do."

Rey Rey called me after she left and asked me to bring her some weed over to the hotel. When I got there she came to the door in a thong and a T-shirt. I asked if that was for me. She said, "Do you want it?" That was like asking a crackhead if he wanted a hit.

I said, "Hell, yeah," so I took my clothes off and we got busy. I was a little late getting back but it was cool—we were not real busy.

After I got off work I went and bought a six-pack of Heineken; then I went over to D's. There was something about her that made me crazy. She had on pajamas and smelled like she had just gotten out of the shower. We were sitting there talking and I pulled out some fonto leaf. She said, "What's that?" I told her that instead of smoking blunts, I use real leaf to roll with. She was impressed and said she liked the way it tasted. She was getting real comfortable with me. She would put her feet on me and start rubbing my leg. I noticed how pretty her feet were, and I just wanted to suck her toes. I did and she liked it. Then she slid over on top of me and started kissing me and slow grinding on me. She would start panting and sighing but she wouldn't have sex with me. I mean, I almost came in my pants. Then she climbed over on her side of the couch. We talked for a minute; then I left. On my way home it came to me that she had used me. I had never experienced that before. All I could do was laugh.

In the meantime there was Evelyn. She was a sales rep from the radio station. She was from Cypress. Her accent really turned me on. One time we were at her apartment having sex. We were doing it doggy style and she started speaking in Greek. I said, "What did you say?"

She said, "Oh, I'm sorry. I called you my superman." I said, "That's OK," and continued.

My life was now so crazy. I was acting just like I did before my first treatment—running around like I was crazy. It's the same old adage: one is too many and a thousand is never enough. I didn't realize how close I was to losing everything I had worked for.

Around Thanksgiving, D decided to move back to Cincy. I went over to her house. That's when I met her mom. We hit it off right away. So I helped her load some things in her car and put some in mine and followed her to Cincy. I remembered thinking, *Why am I doing this? All she wants to do is use me.* So I said, "When we get there, I'll just get the stuff out of the cars and leave." Then she asked me if I wanted to stay awhile. I said sure. We sat down and smoked a joint and drank a beer. Her mom had gone to bed. D went and took a shower. When she came out she said, "Come and sit by me on the floor." She started kissing and rubbing on my penis. I slipped my hand under her robe. She wasn't wearing any panties. I was like, *Oh, snap, this is it.* I said to myself, *It's probably not going to be any good.* She told me to take off my pants. She climbed on top of me and started working. She was talking so nasty. She said, "You like this big pussy, don't you?" She had so much control it felt like she was jacking me off. It felt so good.

Before I knew it, I said, "Uh-oh." I threw my hands up, trying to draw some strength from somewhere and think of something else.

She said, "You a hoe," as she went up for the last time. She was trembling as she slowly slid down my shaft. We came together. It was so nice. We sat there for a minute.

Then I had to drive back to Dayton. I thought, *Why am I doing this just for sex?* It's funny because I had had that same conversation with myself about dope.

One day we were at work sitting in a used car building when Mel came in. I thought that it was so cool. This was the richest man I had ever met. He took the time to sit and talk to us. One thing he said that really stuck was, "There are not many problems that a man can have that money won't take care of." We often had words in passing. He was my idol, but there was a lady there that was the number one salesperson and that's all he could see. She was screwing him over all the time. That kind of reminds me of a story. The birds were flying south for the winter. One bird procrastinated, and as he was flying his wings froze and he crashed through a barn roof. While he was lying there, a cow shit on him. He started to thaw; then a cat came and licked the shit off him and ate him. The moral of this story is that everyone that shits on you isn't your enemy and everyone that kisses your ass isn't your friend.

By this time I was getting out of order. I was running everywhere. I had picked up some customers in Springfield that I was selling pounds to. Plus I had so many women it was wearing me out. I had even started taking them on runs with me just to spend time with them. That has always been a no no. The fewer people that knew what I was doing, the less chance of me getting caught. The worst part is I started having crack cravings and I ignored it. That should have been the first sign to stop what I was doing. I had completely forgotten the pain that I was in six years ago and how God had delivered me. Now I was doing everything I could against God's will. I was full tilt into self-will run riot. My greed and self-centeredness had completely taken over and I couldn't stop.

It was now December 1996. We were getting ready for the dealership Christmas party. This was going to be the blowout of the year and also the start of my demise. We had the party at the Embassy Suites in Cincy. I had a presidential suite and so did the manager. We got all dressed up. This was the first time Donna and I had been out in a while. She was so beautiful. I really did love my wife. I was just caught up in self-obsession. I would chase anything that made me feel good, not caring about anything or anybody else. I had all but forgotten how Donna made me feel. We got to the hotel and took everything in. It seemed like we had enough clothes and liquor for a week. We got to the room; it was a lot nicer than I expected. Donna ran in and went down the hallway into the bedroom. I heard a scream. "We have a Jacuzzi."

I said, "I know. Now bring your ass here and help me with this stuff." As more of the employees got there, they started coming to my room. We were smoking weed and drinking. We were good and tore up by the time the party started. The food and everything was on point. It was beautiful. They had everything we could ever want at the bar, even though we brought our bar with us. There again, my greed had kicked in. After the party, we went back up to the room and drank some more, as if I needed it. Donna went and lay down. I went down to my manager's room. That's when it happened. I went in his bathroom and he was cooking cocaine. My stomach started flipping. I started passing gas. The obsession and compulsion were all over me. I was stone drunk and couldn't resist the craving. So he rolled up a primo and I couldn't wait for him to light it. We were now all sitting out in the sleeping area; it was about four or five of us. I told him to pass me the primo. One of the guys that worked with me knew me from back in the day. He had seen what I went through in the eighties. He said, "Are you sure you want to do that?"

I told him, "One won't hurt me." I had forgotten how greedy I was. That old saying came true. One is too many and a thousand is never enough. That one hit let the gorilla loose. He was all over me. By the time I left his room, I was begging him to sell me some to take back to my room. When I got back to the room, I tried to give Donna some. She freaked. I told her that if she was scared, to go to church. Right then it seemed like I heard a clap of thunder. I had brought damnation on myself.

In the months to come, things got worse—the drinking, the women, everything. I was getting disenchanted with my job. I was thinking about trying to run away from myself again. I was thinking about going to Carolina again.

This was February of 1997. D and I left to go to Carolina. For me it was a business trip as well as pleasure. I took some weed and some cocaine as I did many times before. No one knew that I was coming. That's the way I liked it, just in case they wanted to set me up. This way, I could slip in and out virtually undetected.

We got there and hung out for the weekend. On Monday I got up and went to look for a job. By one o'clock I had a choice of three different jobs. D was amazed. I said, "I'm more than just a pretty face."

We stayed in Charlotte for a couple of nights, Gastonia a couple of nights, and Kings Mountain a couple of nights. Everywhere we went, people thought we were celebrities. People would always stop and talk to us. We even had a waitress sit down at our booth and talk to us. D was outdone by this. I told her people in Carolina were just friendly like that. To me, being dressed like we were and riding in a fly ride were normal. In Charlotte, they weren't used to that unless you were a drug dealer or athlete. Even though I did sell drugs, I didn't look like your typical drug dealer. She said, "Timmy, if one more person stops and talks to us, I am going to scream." We would get high all day and have sex all night. I even took her to her first juke joint. She really got a kick out of that. It was really nice having her in Carolina with me.

When we left Carolina it was snowing. I was supposed to go to work the next day, so I let D drive. She drove most of the way back. When we got to her house, I told her I was going to call in. She got pissed. She said, "Timmy, we could have stayed in a hotel." She loved spending my money. When she found out what I had taken with us, she got even angrier. She said I should have told her I had all those drugs with us so she could have decided if she wanted to go or not. She thought I was just job hunting. Actually, me getting paper was how we were able to do the things we were doing.

When I got home, Donna asked how my trip was. This was getting harder and harder—hiding all the wrong I was doing. I was truly being driven by my greed and self-centeredness. I was truly mentally drained.

I took Donna and the children out to eat. I told them I had gotten a job in Carolina, and I would be going down in March. They could come down when they got out of school. They loved it.

March came. I had moved to Carolina. I started working at Towne and Country Ford. This was the biggest dealership I had ever worked at. They even had a restaurant in the dealership.

One morning when I got to work there was a young lady in there getting some coffee. I shook her hand and introduced myself to her. She had a big, pretty smile and some big, beautiful brown eyes. She had an Explorer in getting some service on it. We talked for a while. She had all my attention and she knew it. She had long, silky hair and a long, lean physique. I mean, she was built like a hooker, but she had the sweetest personality. I found out she was from Memphis. I told her I was from Ohio. She said, "You are one of those Northern redbones."

I said, "If you say so." I told her I had just started working there. I told her how I was having a tough time getting started. You know— planting a seed.

Later that day she called back. She said she just wanted to see how my day was going. I told her it was going pretty good. I told her all I could do was think about her since I met her. I could hear her smiling through the phone. She said, "Sure you have." She told me that she had to go to the spa that night but she wanted to see me. She said that she wanted to do something for me.

I said, "Oh yeah?"

She said, "Yeah." She said, "I will come by and see you tomorrow at lunch; we can go get something to eat."

The next day around noon, I saw her Explorer pull in. I got up from my desk and went out. She got out of her truck. She had on some capris. I said, "Damn, you are sexy." She smiled and put her arms around me and gave me a kiss. Man, she felt like cotton in my arms. She also had some of the softest lips I had ever kissed. I let my hands slide down and cup her ass while I was looking deep into her eyes. It felt even nicer than I imagined.

She said, "Don't do that out here." I apologized. I told her I got a little carried away. She didn't have time to go eat. Something came up. She said, "Take this," and handed me a bank envelope. It felt kind of thick. I didn't open it right then. She said, "I wish I could do more, but that should help until you get paid." I told her I wasn't expecting anything. She said, "I know. I just wanted to help." I said thank you and pulled her to me and gave her a long, sensuous kiss.

I let my hand slide down and cup her ass again. She said, "Boy, you better quit."

I thought, *Damn, this ass is soft.*

She said, "You have the nicest lips." I told her she hadn't seen anything yet.

I went back to my desk and opened the envelope. It had $280 in it. I thought, *Now, what the hell is she wanting?* I thought that was kind of fast. By the time I got off work she had called me and wanted me to come by. I said OK. She gave me directions and I told her I would see her at about nine thirty.

When I got there, she had dinner cooked and was walking around in a silk robe and some house shoes. I could tell she wasn't wearing any panties, because there weren't any panty lines. I knew she didn't have on a bra because her nipples were showing. She had the sexiest legs I had seen since I left Cincy. I was sitting there trying to keep it together. She just turned me on so much; plus she could cook. We had nice conversation and the food was good also.

I went over and sat down to watch TV. I asked for an ashtray. She said she didn't smoke. I later found that she didn't drink either. She sat down beside me. As we were talking she starting rubbing my leg. Then she said, "Is something wrong?" looking at the bulge in my pants.

I said, "Why do you ask?" Then she stroked it with her fingertips and she said, "You just seem a little excited."

I said, "Maybe a little." Then she pulled it out and got on her knees in front of me. Her long, silky hair was draped over my pelvic area.

As she slid my pants down, I said, "You know this is rape?"

She said, "You can't rape the willing." Then she continued giving me head while she was helping me get my pants off. When she got my pants off, she climbed on top. Man, she felt so good. We had sex I know for a couple of hours. I was so tired when we finished I fell dead asleep. I woke up the next morning and went home.

I was off work that day. Evelyn called me and said she was going to Greenville, South Carolina, to see another friend of ours. She asked how far it was from Kings Mountain. I told her, "About eighty miles." She said she would really love to see me. So I said, "Why don't you fly into Charlotte and I will come and get you?"

She said, "Cool." I sat around that day. I finally got out and cut the grass and did some things around the house. Then my dad came home. I could see that he was happy to see me, but he had a look of concern. He asked me where I had been. I told him where I had been.

He just shook his head and said, "You better be careful." He said, "You don't know what these woman have going on. They could be telling you anything."

And I explained to him how I check them out real good before I go to sleep there. I said, "Dad, game can recognize game."

He just laughed and said, "OK." Then he walked away.

My addiction had started to kick back in also. I still couldn't seem to get to a meeting. I was too caught up in everything else. I had picked up a couple other women. I was really running wild and my judgment was getting bad also.

So after a week or so, Evelyn called and said she was coming in and she wanted me to pick her up.

She made the trip and I went and picked her up. I let her drive to Greenville. On the ride to Greenville, I had some time to think. I thought about where I was going and where I had been. The space I was in was starting to feel real familiar, and it wasn't feeling very good. It was starting to feel like the mid- to late eighties, when I was starting to lose control over my drug use; how it was covered up by the money I was getting, and the women. When the money was gone I was in a pit so deep it took an act of God to get me out. Then Evelyn turned the music down. She said, "I thought you would never let anyone drive this car—not your pride and joy. What's wrong with you?" I told her I was just tired. I didn't want to tell her that I was doing drugs again. I knew I would never be able to get another dime out of her—not that that was the only reason I was seeing her. It had to be something more than that to attract me in the first place.

Soon Donna and the children moved down. We stayed for a year. Things were getting progressively worse. At the time, I had a green Mark VIII. It was the fastest, sweetest ride I ever had—I mean, from the Dayton wire wheels to the three-thousand-watt stereo. Like Evelyn said, it was my pride and joy.

I worked in Gaffney, South Carolina, and lived in Kings Mountain. They were twenty miles apart. One morning I made it to work in about twelve minutes. I ran between 110 and 140 miles per hour the whole way. I called Donna when I got to work. She couldn't believe that I had made it already. She went off on me. She asked if I was trying to kill myself. At the time I really didn't know. We used to service the highway patrol cars. The next day one of the troopers came in and said he had seen me on 85. He said if he thought he could have caught me, he would have taken me to jail. Donna worked third shift, so it made it kind of easy for me to do what I wanted. The only thing I wanted to do was get high. I was right back in the hole I was in seven and a half years ago.

I noticed my judgment was getting bad when I started messing with the preacher's wife. She was so fine though. She was built like Jessica Rabbit. When she came into the dealership, it seemed like time stopped. She had long, thick, curly hair that just bounced when she walked. She worked at a gospel radio station. I even hit it there once. We would go out to lunch. She was getting hotels. I mean, she was starting to get real crazy. Her husband called me at work one day. I said, "Well, I guess that's it." If that would have kept up, someone would have gotten hurt.

This was now spring 1998. Evelyn called and said she was in Greenville. I had gotten high earlier and I really needed to get away. Tim and Nikki were over at my dad's. I took Antonio and hit the road. I just had to go. I would figure out what to tell them later. I told Antonio we were going to see some friends in Greenville. That's the same thing I told Donna when I called her at work.

We got there. Evelyn and Jane and Jane's husband took to Antonio instantly—mainly because he was my son, beside the fact that he was a nice-looking boy and well-mannered also.

We kicked it for a minute, watching movies and stuff. Then I put Antonio to bed. I stayed up for a while talking. I had to tell someone what was going on. I felt like I could trust them, but at this time it didn't matter. I had to just get it off of me. That's one thing I learned from going to NA—pain shared is pain lessened. They had a lot of compassion for me. I felt like they truly cared. I told them about the drugs. I couldn't tell Evelyn about the women. I didn't want to hurt her. As it turned out, she was mad at me because I didn't sleep with her. Yeah, I hit it, but I didn't want Antonio to wake up and I not be in the bed with him. I had to keep that cool.

As I look back, I can see how God was working in my life. Even though I was going through some tough times, he was pricking my spirit and letting me see the error of my ways. He was allowing me to get enough pain to draw me closer to him. All of a sudden I wasn't feeling so good about what I was doing. I made a decision that this would be the last time I would see Evelyn like this. Antonio and I left the next day and went home. I felt refreshed. I thought I would be able to stop using. I was just lying to myself.

When I got home, Donna was there and we sat and talked. I told her that we went to see Jane and her husband. I didn't mention Evelyn. I was so tired of keeping all these secrets. I can see now that was a big part of my problem—the guilt and shame.

It wasn't long before Donna gave me that look. I said, "What?"

She said, "You know what." So I went and got some dope. We did what we do—smoking and having sex. I can't blame it on her. We were both sick. I wanted to stop but I just couldn't. I had come to the conclusion that we were no good for each other. I don't know what kept me coming back. It's like I was under a spell.

We were losing everything. I figured it was time to go home. I called Adam. He was my general manager at Mel Farr Lincoln-Mercury. I told him things weren't working out too good. He said, "Come on home, brother." That made me feel good—to know I had a job waiting for me.

I called my mother and told her that we needed to come home and we needed a place to stay. She sent my brothers and another friend of ours to help us move. This was the summer of 1998. We got all moved in, and it wasn't long before the craziness started.

I went to work. I asked myself, *What the hell did I get myself into?* The dealership was in such a wreck, there were $250,000 worth of repos on the back lot. It was up to us to try and sell them. It was so funny—when Mel was coming to town, it looked like a bunch of roaches scampering around, trying to get all the cars off the back lot so he wouldn't see them. The person that he had given so much praise to, turned out to be the one screwing him over all the time. Remember that story about the birds flying south. That never rings more true than here.

Things were getting crucial for me. I was about to lose my cars. So I quit Mel Farr and went back to Fairborn Buick so I could get a demo to drive. That job didn't last long either. I got tired of the pay plan and decided I could do better. I turned in my keys to my demo and got a ride home. It wasn't long before I had another job. God was real good to me in that aspect, although my life was still torn up.

It was spring 1999. I had been working at another dealership for a while. Now things were starting to go pretty good. We were setting all kinds of records. I was making good money. I had even managed to get a couple of cars. Things were getting better in my life. I had given up chasing women. I wasn't getting high as much. I was really trying to quit. I was trying to get closer to God. The closer I got, the better things would get. I knew I needed the Lord in my life and I was really trying to get there. I had just one problem: drugs.

By the year 2000 things were getting crazy again—no women, just drugs. People in my family started dropping like flies. First it was my grandmother; this was my dad's mom. She would have been 101 if she would have lived until her birthday. I had no idea as to what would follow. That summer, five people in my family died between June and September. This would be a major turning point in my life.

My cousin Frances died in June. We were over at her brother's house after the funeral, as black folks do. We were drinking and playing cards. My phone rang. It was one of my cats. I wasn't even thinking about getting high. He asked me what was going on. I told him what was up. He asked me if I needed anything. I told him I didn't have any money. He said, "You know I got you; what do you want?"

I said, "Fuck it, give me a 50." He said he was getting ready to go out of town. He said all he had was a $100 piece and to come and get it. So that's what I did.

That's the way things worked out for me in Dayton. For years I had a reputation for doing what I said I would do. If I owed you money, you got paid; if I told you I was going to do you, you were done.

In July my aunt Liz died. This is when I realized how bad I really was. I had got off work and stopped and got some dope. When I got home they called and said everyone was at the hospital because Aunt Liz had passed. My emotions were so numb from smoking dope, I didn't even want to go to the hospital. Donna said she would come and get me. I finished what I had by the time she got there. All I could think about on the way to the hospital was how I could get some money to get some more dope. When we got there, I couldn't show any emotions and I still didn't associate it with the drugs. I know now that I was truly caught up and I hope she forgives me. I know she's up there somewhere, looking down on me and wanting the best for me. For the rest of my days I'm going to do my best to be the man that she would want me to be.

A few days later we had the funeral. That's when all my emotions surfaced. I just exploded in tears and sorrow—the memories of her and how I was so ashamed of how I was acting. My aunt truly loved me. If no one else did, I know Aunt Liz did.

So after the funeral we went over my cousin Jesse's. Jesse was her son. My brother and one of my cousins and I drank a half gallon of brandy. I was so drunk. Now I wanted a hit of crack, so I called one of my cats. He said he was at the VFW. I said, "Cool. I'm on my way." So my dumb ass gets there and starts drinking some more. I guess I wasn't quite drunk enough. He gave me a half gram of powder. I took it, but it wasn't what I wanted. I left and went by a dope spot that I frequented. They didn't have anything. When I left, I didn't notice the police behind me. They pulled me over at Third and Gettysburg. I forgot about the powder in my pocket. When they searched me that's what they found. That's probably what kept me from getting a DUI. They figured they had enough on me. They took me to jail and charged me with possession—a fifth-degree felony. This was the first time I had ever been busted. Thank God that's all it was. They informed me that I couldn't bond out on a felony. I had to see the judge on Monday morning.

Monday came and I went to court. I was so embarrassed going into court in that orange jumpsuit. I said, "What the hell. Here we go." This is when they hit me with the charge. My brother and his wife were there. This made it worse, but what could I do? It was not as bad as I thought. They gave me a court date and released me on an OR bond. My brother waited on me to give me a ride home. My own wife wasn't even there. It's like she didn't even care.

We talked, and he laughed and said, "You looked real cute in orange."

I said, "Did it turn you on or something?" We just laughed.

He said, "You better be glad that's all it was and not some of that other stuff you have been doing."

The time came for me to go to court. The judge asked me if I had an attorney. I told her that I didn't need one, I pled guilty. She said, "Slow down, Mr. Sawyer. There are some other things we have got to do first." First, I had to go to the public defender's office to get a lawyer. I could have got one on my own. I wasn't going to spend money to be found guilty. So I got the public defender. I pled guilty. They put me on the TLC program—treatment in lieu of conviction—which gave me six months of probation. They sent me to the probation office to get signed up.

My probation started when I got down there. I saw all the hotties they had as POs. Isn't that something—in trouble and still thinking about women? I had hoped I would get one of them. Instead, I got a man. It seemed like he had it out for me from the get go. I couldn't see it was me with the problem. After a bunch of PVs—probation violations—and nights in jail, I got tired. I knew they were going to give me the time I had on the shelf, so I checked myself into treatment to dodge it. This pissed my probation officer off. I could tell. I said, "Fuck him. This is my life."

So he pulled me out of the place where I was and sent me to the VOA in Cincy. I was supposed to do four months there. This was the craziest place I had ever seen. This was a halfway house for sex offenders, parolees, and probationers. There was all kinds of stuff going on in there. There were people smoking crack in the showers. People were jumping out of the window, going to get beer and bringing it back. It was crazy. It amazed me that I didn't have a desire to participate in any of it—especially the smoking crack. There were a couple of guys that tried me while I was there. I didn't want to get in trouble, so I prayed. That was my first physical evidence of God working in my life. The one guy got caught having sex with another guy in the freight elevator. The other guy got caught for being drunk. That showed me that if I would be still, the Lord would fight my battles.

Here I was back in Cincy again. I stayed there and finished my treatment. The first month was treatment. The other three months was like being in a halfway house. It was near Christmastime, so I got a job at Wal-Mart. Within a month they put me in the management training program. This was a blessing because it gave me more time out of that nut house.

After a while, they found out I had a car at VOA and they called me into the office. I knew this was against the rules, but I did it anyway. When I figured out they were going to make me lose my job, I left and went to a friend of mine's transitional house. I called my probation officer the next day and told him what I had done. He got pissed and said that I had better be in Dayton for drug court Friday. I knew he was going to put some shit in the game, so I went up early and talked to the judge that was running drug court. I showed him my certificate that I got from completing treatment, and told him that I had moved out of the VOA into a transitional house. I told him that I had gotten a career job and they were going to make me lose it. He told me that he understood what I did, but he didn't like the way I went about it. He said I had showed some responsibility in owning up to what I did, so he said he would roll with it. I asked him what about the PO. He said he would take care of that. That's God working again.

When I got back to court, I could see the PO was mad enough to spit fire, but there was nothing he could do. He called me in the hallway to talk to me. He told me he had planned to put me in the VOA in Dayton, but God nixed that plan. He had a smirk like he could just kill me. He gave me my new schedule and sent me on my way.

During this time I joined a church in Cincy called the Beams of Heaven Baptist Church. When I got my job at Wal-Mart, a guy that worked there was a member of the church. It started out with us talking about music. He told me he was a bass player. He told me that he played for the church. I told him I was a bass player also. He invited me to church with him. I said I would come. I was really trying to improve my relationship with God.

I got to church. He introduced me as one of his guests. Then he put me on the spot—he invited me up to play for devotional. It seemed as though he was trying to embarrass me, but it backfired on him. Even though I hadn't played for a while, I still played better than he did. I could see that it was totally unexpected. I guess he thought I was lying about playing the bass. He rushed and grabbed his guitar from me. I later found out that he had a very jealous spirit. I ended up taking his place playing for the church.

As I walked back to my seat, a vision of loveliness walked in. I mean, she was so damn fine. It seemed like I heard the angels singing. We made eye contact and smiled at each other. It was a mutual attraction. De was her name. She was so fine—nice height, about five foot seven, 135 to 140 pounds, such a lovely face, beautiful complexion, pretty eyes and lips. She had the total package, I thought. I just had to have her.

After church I found out that the pastor and one of the deacons knew my parents. We all went to Frisch's after church. I asked her if I could sit with her. She said sure. We sat at a booth. I sat across from her. She was so beautiful. I couldn't keep my eyes off her. As we sat and talked, I noticed how I would say something, then she would laugh and say, "I was just thinking that." Then she said something that I was thinking. I had never experienced something like this happening before. I asked her when her birthday was. It was June 22nd—the same as my sister's and nine days before mine. She told me her ankle was hurting. I told her to put it up on the bench and I would rub it. She laughed and said, "Oh, no. We aren't going to start that." We exchanged numbers and went our separate ways. I couldn't wait to talk to her.

I told the guys back at the house about her. They said, "If you are talking like that about her now, I would hate for her to give you some sex."

This was the first woman I had hooked up with since I had been in treatment. I had all these feelings and emotions coming out and I couldn't control them. I had insecurity problems. I knew that I didn't have a lot to offer. She was so fine, she could have any guy she wanted. I just didn't trust her. I wanted to control the relationship, but that wasn't going to happen. There was just too much going on. I was still married and she had babies daddy drama. Isn't that something?

One Sunday, the church had to go to fellowship with another church in Dayton. I called Donna and told her to bring the kids. This was tense.

Shortly after we got there, Donna and the children pulled up. We had already put the equipment in the church. I came back outside. A few of the church members were standing outside along with De. I introduced them to my children and Donna. Donna was looking good also. We went in and sat down. When the choir got up to sing, the preacher acknowledged my family. This made me feel weird. Everyone in our church knew that I liked De, and my wife was there. I knew this just didn't look right.

We sang and were leaving the church. Donna gave me a kiss. I just knew De was watching. Sure enough, when I got on the bus, it seemed as if De's eyes would have been blades, I wouldn't be writing this book. That look she gave me really hurt. I guess my feelings were getting deeper than I thought. When I took my seat, I called her cell phone. I couldn't wait until we got back. I couldn't sit with her—that just wouldn't have looked good. When she answered, the first thing she said was, "I saw that kiss." She tried to act like it didn't matter. She said, "That's the reason I didn't want to mess with you in the first place." Then she said, "I want to get off the phone now," and she hung up.

Because I was concentrating so hard on De, once again I forgot about my recovery. Once again sex had taken the place of what I was supposed be doing in the first place. Even though I met her in church, the devil was still trying to destroy me through her. My being so caught up in her contributed to me being put out of the transitional house. She was so intoxicating. When we made love it was like I was in another world. To this day, I still have a special place in my heart for her.

The guys at the house were getting jealous because of my relationship with De. She was finer than anybody they could ever hope to be with. I had a lot of other stuff going on also. Now I was selling cars again. I was really making loot. I was sharp every day. I had two cars there. They thought the house manager was playing favorites. Come to find out he was just as jealous as they were. For some reason it made them feel less than.

One weekend I had gone out and had not paid my rent. The manager said if we had not paid our rent that we were not to leave. I had already talked to the owner and told him that I had the money. I tried to give it to him when I got back and he wouldn't take it. He told me I had to leave. I called De and told her what happened. She said I could come stay with her. I could tell she was reluctant and later I found out why. Her baby's daddy was still stalking her. She didn't want any problems with him. She said that there was nothing happening between the two of them. The sex was so good, and she was so fine, I could see how it could make a weak-minded brother do some crazy things. Believe me, I was just hanging on by a thread.

She starting saying I needed to find some place to stay. Right then my whole attitude changed. If she couldn't be down for me in the bad times, I sure as hell was not going to be around in the good times.

At the end of the week I moved in with a guy that I worked with at the dealership. This was a trip. I had never lived with a white guy before. I knew this would not last long, because his girl had him tripping. They were supposed to be broken up, but she would come and go as she pleased. They had two bad-ass kids that were not disciplined at all. This made it very uncomfortable.

In the meantime I sold this girl an Explorer. She was coming on to me pretty hard. I was still kind of pissed off at De. I said, "What the hell." Regi and I kicked it for a while. She just wasn't De.

Soon I got so frustrated, I started drinking more. One night I bought a bottle. After I got good and tipsy, my cravings came back. Then I wanted a hit. I got dressed and went to Brandy's nightclub. I sat there and drank some more. I said, "Fuck it. I'm going to Dayton and get some dope." I did not even think of trying to get it in Cincy. I really didn't know anyone to get it from.

I left the club and headed for the highway and got pulled over. I truly believe the sheriff saved my life. As drunk as I was, I probably would not have made it to Dayton. This was God doing for me what I could not do for myself.

I dodged another DUI because I had a capias in Golf Manor for an allowing drug abuse charge that I never paid the fine for. Instead of giving me a ticket, the sheriff called the Golf Manor police and had them come get me. I guess he did not want to deal with the paperwork. So the Golf Manor police got there and took me to the station. He told me if I could come up with $320 I could go. I called De on her cell phone to see if she could help me out. As I was talking to her, I heard a guy ask, "Where are you ladies going?" She said she and her girlfriend had gone out and she did not know who the guy was that came up to the car. You know, I didn't believe that shit. This made me feel worse. I felt like someone had just cut my heart out. I was truly in love with that girl. After I could not come up with the money, they took me to the Hamilton County justice center (jail). This was my first trip there. I stayed there until Monday. As a last resort, I called Donna and she came and got me. It seems no matter how many jams I had been in, Donna had always been there for me. Through all the other women, treatment centers, and just total neglect of spending time with her, I had started to wonder if she was letting me run so she could run. You know that old song, "Who's making love to your old lady while you were out making love?" I guess the player was starting to die. I never used to think about that before. We went and got my clothes and got my car out of impound, and back to Dayton I went. I always seemed to end up right back where I started. I loved being with my children. They were the only bright spot in my life. Although I loved Donna, we seemed not to be able to get past our addiction.

It was now spring of 2001. It was not hard for me to find a new job or drug connection. It was not long before we were right back where we started. I believe the sexual things that we would do while we were getting high were as big of an addiction as the drugs themselves.

I used to love taking a hit and while I had smoke in my mouth suck on her vagina and lick on her clit while she was taking a hit. Then she would get on top of me and ride it. She would come so much and get so wet. We would go on like this for hours. It's kind of like that comedy skit that Richard Pryor used to do. He said, "You think of the freakiest stuff when you do cocaine." He said, "I'm going to run around the house three times and on the third time I want you to jump off on my face." It got to the point it seemed we could not have sex without drugs. This went on for a while—too long.

On Thanksgiving we went to Kocomo, Indiana. A college friend of Donna's had invited us up to spend the holiday with her family. We went up and had a nice time. I got to know her husband pretty well. Donna and I had talked about moving there—here we go again. We were trying to run from our problems when it was us all along.

I was working at Peffley Ford in Dayton. Business was very slow. Even my son said, "Dad, when are you going to get another job? Peffley's just is not cutting it." I stayed there for about another month or so. I had called over to Indianapolis to check out some dealers. This was January 2002. I ended up going to interview with Paul Harvey Ford on a Friday. He asked if I could start that Saturday.

I said, "Sure," and I went by Donna's friend's house and asked if I could stay for about a month. They said that would be fine. I left and went to get some clothes, and went off to Indianapolis.

My first day there I sold three cars. I thought this would be great. I was used to knowing how much I made on my deals right then. They seemed to be reluctant to tell me. I started getting a real strange feeling. One of the other salespeople told me, "Veteran salespeople don't stay here long," and I found out why. They were robbing the salespeople blind.

About my third week I asked my manager what was going on. He told me he wasn't going to have me questioning every deal. He said if I didn't trust him he didn't need me on his lot. I said, "You're firing me?"

He said, "Yes, get off my lot." This was the start of my demise. It took two months for me to get another job. I was blackballed.

In the meantime I had joined a church and they were helping me. Instead of me getting closer to God, the devil was pulling me the other way.

One of my friends in Carolina had gotten killed in a car accident—Barry, the guy that moved to Oklahoma City with me. It was weird because his father-in-law had passed that morning at about 6 a.m. By noon Barry and his brother-in-law had gotten killed in a car accident. My brother and I went to the funeral. When we pulled up in my dad's yard, they said, "Tim, telephone."

I said to myself, *Damn, let me get in town first.* It was Minny. My cousin Ruby had told her I was coming. That was perfect timing.

Later I went over to her house. When I pulled up in her driveway, she had a Lexus LS400 and a Nissan 300ZX. I was like, damn, things must be good. I went in and we talked for a minute. Then we started kissing and one thing led to another and before I knew it we were in bed. I really put on a clinic. When we were finished, we lay there and talked. She asked me what we were going to do Saturday. I told her Mike was planning on going out. But I had only brought a suit for the funeral. She said when she got off work she would come and get me.

So I got back to my dad's house after we had breakfast. We sat and talked for a minute. Then we went and did some visiting. My cousins were down from Pennsylvania. We all knew Barry; he was like another brother to us.

So that evening Minny called. She said she was on her way. When she got there, we went and got a room and then we went to the mall. She really laid me out. They had suits there I had never seen anywhere. She bought me this bad-ass Stacey Adams hookup.

I mean, suit, shirt, tie, socks, and shoes—the whole nine. Then we headed back to Kings Mountain. We stopped at the liquor store on the way back to my dad's. My sister called me on my cell phone. She said my son was asking where I was. She was complaining about me leaving him with my dad. My son dearly loves his grandfather. So I said, "Put Tim on the phone." I said, "Tim, are you OK?" He said yes. I asked him if he wanted something. He told me to bring him some chips. I said, "OK. I will be there in a minute."

When I got back to my dad's, I let my sister have it. I told her she need not ever tell me about leaving my son with his grandfather. I told her she had never raised her children. If my mom did not have them, my aunt Liz had them. My stepmom was like Tim. She wanted me to stop. I was dropping bombs and the bad part is it was all true.

So after things got calmed down a bit, Minny and I went and got a hotel room. While we were getting ready to go out, you know I had to hit it for a minute. You know—thank her for the clothes. I thanked her so well, she said she was almost too weak to go out. We went to the Excelsior Club in Charlotte. It was a gang of us. Mary and I were in her Lexus; my brother and my cousins were behind us. There were so many fine women there, but Minny was just as fine, so it didn't faze me one bit. We had a really good time. We left and went back to the hotel. I hit it again and went to bed. Minny was about thirteen years older than me. She would just keep putting it on me until she passed out.

The next day we went to the funeral. I had never seen that many people at a funeral in my life. They had all three of them together. They had it at the high school. I saw so many people that I had not seen in forever. I was a good boy. I didn't say anything out of the way to not one woman.

I got back to Indy and did my normal—went job hunting and sat around. Minny called me to see how I was doing. I told her I wasn't doing too good. I was kind of depressed. I had left everything behind to try and start a new life and then this happens.

She told me how when you're trying to do something good, how evil is always lurking in the shadows. She asked me what I needed and I told her whatever she could do would be appreciated.

Later that week I got a letter from Minny. She told me how she missed me. She wished I would move back to Carolina. I wouldn't have anything to worry about. She said she would always have a special place in her heart for me. She said she remembered the first time we met—how I was this mannish teenager that took her by storm and stole her heart. How she saw me grow into a hell of a man that stood strong through adversity that she had seen take so many black men down. She said, "You are still the best lover I know." She said, "Here is $250. I hope it helps. I'll try to send something else later." This really cheered me up. After all these years and all the wrong I'd done, someone still loved me unconditionally. I really feel Minny will always have a special place in my heart even though we will probably never be together again.

Later that day I got a bottle and went over to one of my cats' cribs. We sat over there, drank, and smoked some killer weed. After a while, some of the other cats came over. We decided to go out. I took my car over to one of his other friends' apartments and rode with my boy. I should have left my car at his house. I don't know what the hell I was thinking.

We got to the club. It was packed. There were so many women there I was like a kid in a candy store. We had a few drinks and sat around talking shit. Then I hit the dance floor. I was feeling extra good this night for some reason. Maybe I was still high from Minny's letter. I'm out there dancing. I spot this girl at the bar checking a brother out. After the song went off, I went and grabbed her. Man, this girl was thick. I mean, tits and ass for days. I mean, she was like something straight out of Mississippi. I mean, she had country curves. She kind of reminded me of Oprah accept a little shorter.

We went to the dance floor. We danced to a fast song. Then a slow tune came on. She wasn't trying to go anywhere and neither was I. She told me her name was T. I said, "I bet you are a terror."

She said, "T, not terror."

I said, "Same thing."

She laughed and said, "You are so silly."

I told her, "That's just one of the things you will learn to love about me." Man, she felt good in my arms. So out it came—"Would you like to go home with me?"

She said, "I don't know you like that." I said, "I don't know you either. We are both adults and you seem safe to me. I'm willing to take a chance if you are." Man, the rap was just flowing.

She looked at me and said, "OK." I was like, yesssssss!!!!

By this time the club was getting ready to close. My partner and the other cats were standing near the dance floor waiting on me. I told them I was going with T. They were like, damn, this is your first time here. How are you going to leave with someone and we don't? I just shrugged my shoulders and we left.

When we left, T was walking in front of me. I couldn't keep my eyes off her ass and her bowlegs. She was thick but tight—not a jiggle anywhere. I said to myself, *This is going to be fun.* We got in her car. She asked where my apartment was. I told her she would have to take me to my car first. She asked me where it was. I told her I would have to show her. The truth is, I was so drunk I could barely remember. In fact, I dozed off a couple of times. She said, "Are you going to be alright?"

I said, "Sure. Just get me to my car." So we finally found my car. Then she followed me to my house.

We got to my house and went in. She said, "These are nice apartments."

I said, "Thanks. Sorry I don't have any living room furniture. All I have is a waterbed and a TV."

She said, "That's fine. You have to start somewhere." I asked her if she wanted a drink. She said, "No, thanks." She'd had enough. So I took her by the hand and led her to the bedroom. I sat her on the bed while kissing her and slipping her skirt off as she sat down. I gently slipped her panties off. She didn't say stop, so I knew it was on. I parted her legs ever so gently to reveal her lusciousness. Then I planted my lips right where I knew she'd like it, and she did. She said, "Oh shit, Tim." Then she lay back on the bed. The movement of the bed kept pushing that vagina to me. I kept putting my tongue deeper inside her. Then I would slowly pull it out and try to knock that little man out of the boat. Then I sucked it. I had to grab her to keep her from jumping out of the bed. Then she screamed and the trembling started. Then I gave her the wood. Then she really started throwing it. We went on for about an hour. She started saying stuff like, "Damn, Tim, I can feel your strength," as I stroked it long and slow. Then her legs went straight up in the air and started shaking. She let out one big scream. Then it was over. I just collapsed on top of her, sweating my ass off. I hadn't had a workout like this since forever. We held each other for a while. Then she said she had to go.

I told her, "No, you don't."

She said, "Are you sure?"

I said, "You might as well wait until sunup."

She said, "OK." Then we lay there and went to sleep.

Time went on. I finally got a job, but it was too late. I got evicted from my apartment. Everything that turned out so promising turned to crap. I had gone back to the club. This time I was by myself. I had gotten a little buzzed. Then I had the thought, *A hit would be nice.* All of a sudden I had forgotten the reason I moved to Indy in the first place. All alone with my thoughts sinking into my sorrow, I said the addicts' national anthem: "Fuck it."

I looked around the club to see if I could see someone that looked like they might know something. Sure enough, I ran into a girl and her friend. They just looked like some girls that walked on the wild side. We talked for a minute; then I asked what was going on in town. She said, "What do you want to go on?"

I said, "Whatever." She said, "You want to party?" She asked, "Are you the police?"

I laughed and said, "Hell no."

She said, "Let's go."

I went back to my apartment and got some money. We went to her place and it was on. She called her people. They came over and brought the goods. She cooked it up on the stove. I was trying to rub on her a little while she was cooking. She brushed me off. She said it wasn't that type of party. She said, "Everything around here cost." I knew right then that this was not going to work. She was semi-attractive, but her personality was all jacked up. She was also broke. I probably could have gotten next to her, but that would have taken too much work. And for what—someone to get high with? I think not. That was the problem with Donna and me. So we smoked the dope. I went home and nothing had changed. In fact, it got worse. I was still evicted, plus I was jonesing.

The next week I moved in with my partner. I was glad because I really did not want to be alone. I had even gone to Cincy to pick up D one weekend, which was crazy when I had T right there in Indy. I could see how D still had a hold on me. I could see how the bad decisions and unmanageability were starting to creep back in.

Well, my job wasn't going too good. My partner was hinting about how he really liked living alone. I said, "What the hell. I might as well move back to Dayton," and that's what I did.

So now I'm back in Dayton. I have to start all over again. I had been there before, so it really didn't bother me. What did bother me was Donna's new connections. I had started to wonder if she ever had to fuck them to get some drugs. We were back in the same old cycle.

I got a job at Middletown Ford. This job didn't last long. I was driving twenty-five miles to make the same money I was making at Peffley before I went to Indy. I'd heard about a dealership in Springfield which was the same distance away from home—just the other direction—and they were selling cars.

After a month or so, I went for an interview. As I drove on the lot, I realized I had had a dream about being at this dealership while I was in Indy.

I went in and filled out an application and gave my resume to one of the managers. He and I sat down and talked. I didn't get a very good vibe from him. It was like he was thinking, *Who does this nigga think he is?* I left and called back and asked to speak to the owner. I talked to one of the owners and told him I had been up there and filled out an application, and left my resume. He said he would find it and call me back. After a few hours he called me back. He said he liked what he had seen. He asked if I could come up tomorrow at 9:00 a.m. I said, "I will see you then."

I got there at 9:00 a.m. The man I was supposed to see had not gotten there yet, so I talked to one of the other managers. He practically begged me to stay and talk to the owner, which I was going to do anyway. The owner finally came and we talked for about twenty minutes. He asked me when I wanted to start. I told him immediately. We shook hands and I left.

This was July 7, 2002—the start of a new era. This was feeling so right.

It was not long before I was breaking all kinds of records, making all kinds of bonuses, and—yes—making all kinds of money. While this was good, it made things worse at home. Donna and I just got high more. That is about what it amounted to.

While I was working in Springfield, I got in touch with my old friend Ricky. This is the other guy at one time that I used to sell pounds of weed to. He'd had a kidney transplant, so he wasn't doing too good. This one day, we were sitting there talking and his nurse came by. It was something about her that turned me on. She was tall, brown-skinned, had a short haircut, and talked very intelligently. Plus she had freak written all over her. Her name was Gina—this was Gina #2.

Meanwhile, back at the ranch. This was September 2002. Things were getting worse between Donna and me. We were getting high every day. I was starting to hate it. I felt trapped. I had tried moving away time and time again. It felt like I had a spell on me that kept drawing me back. I started feeling trapped and I didn't like it.

Ricky passed around the end of September or the first of October of 2002. It was a sad occasion, but it got me in touch with Gina #2 again. I know it was bad trying to pick up a chick at a funeral, but I had met her months before and just had to have her. After the funeral we went and ate over at one of Ricky's brothers' houses. Then we went back over to Ricky's. I was sitting there talking to Ricky's wife. Then Gina came in. She was kind of loud, but she wasn't obnoxious, so it was OK. Plus she seemed kind of smart. As time went on she started to seem kind of strange. She had a nice butt; she was an Amazon-type chick. She was sitting on the cooler and I told her she'd better get up before she melted the ice. I was teasing her, but she took offense to it. I was like, oh hell. I tried to get her to take me home with her. She said, "I can't believe that you would try to go home with me the first night." So I gave her a hug and a peck on the cheek and told her goodnight and went home.

After a few weeks went by, Gina called me at work. She asked me if I wanted to have lunch. I said sure. We met at a Chinese Buffet. We sat and talked for a minute and had lunch. She asked me if I wanted to go to a Halloween party with her. I said I could probably swing that. She said, "I don't know if you are ready for this. The people that are giving the party are gay. And there will probably be a bunch of gay people there." I told her that as long as they didn't bother me, I would be OK. So we finished eating. I went back to work and sold a couple of cars—you know, did what I do.

I got home. The children were doing their thing. Donna had that look like she was trying to get high. By this time, I was really tired of getting high. All I wanted to do was get away. I told her I was going out and I left. I got over to Gina's. She had a nice house. We sat down and had a drink. Then she got dressed and we left.

We got to the party. This was some of the funniest stuff I had ever seen in my life. I had never been to a party with a bunch of gay people before. When we got there, Gina said, "This is my man, and you queens leave him alone."

I said to myself, *Oh shit.* They were cool though. I had so much fun. It wasn't anything like I expected. They made little comments, but it was all in fun.

By the middle of November, right before Thanksgiving, life was getting unbearable with Donna. She wasn't happy and neither was I.

I moved in with Gina. I told her I just needed a few weeks so I could get my own place. At this time we hadn't had sex yet. I felt kind of good about that. I told Donna I was staying with a guy that I worked with. I didn't like doing this, but I didn't know what else to do. I was trying to save my life. I was really good at running. They say that sometimes a good run is better than a bad stand.

The first night was cool. We sat and talked and she fixed me dinner. She even ironed my clothes for work the next day. She still tried to play hard to get. I told her I was tired and asked her to get some sheets and a blanket so I could sleep on the couch. I got the couch all made up and got my clothes off and lay down. Gina went and took a bath. I assumed she was going to bed. I had dozed off. The next thing I knew she had lain on top of me. She was giving me little kisses and rubbing my head. It startled me at first. Then I wrapped my arms around her and gave her a deep, sensual kiss. Man, she went off. I thought she was coming right then. She wasn't though. She was just hot as hell. I stuck my finger in her vagina; she was wet as hell. Then we made love right there on the couch. She rode me and I rode her, and it was good too.

Gina was really nice and so were her people. I went over to her mom and dad's for Thanksgiving. They welcomed me with open arms. They had so much food. Gina and I went back to the house. I took a shower and got in bed—she had a nice, big bed, one of those that were made for a canopy, but it didn't have one. It was high too. It felt like it was about five feet tall and had the nicest mattress I ever lay on.

She got out of the tub and came to bed. She was still kind of wet. I dried her back off and took lotion and started rubbing her down. I said to myself I was going to turn her out. I gave her a nice massage as I lotioned her down. Then I slid up against her with my legs straddling her and hanging off the bed. Then I got some more lotion on my hands. Then I reached around and started rubbing her breasts and stomach. I starting kissing her neck and down her back. She leaned her head back and starting kissing me. It was so warm and sensuous. I could feel the warm smoothness of her freshly lotioned back against my chest. Her warm, soft lips and tongue against mine.

We were really getting heated. Then I laid her back and slid around on top and started gently kissing her breasts. Then I slowly worked my way down to her stomach. I played with her belly button for a minute. This must have tickled, because she giggled like a little girl. By the time I made it to her valley of love, her body was jumping like bacon in a skillet. I played with her clit for a little while; then I stuck my tongue inside. She was so hot and sweet too. Then I pulled my tongue out and started sucking on her clit. Then I stuck my finger in her vagina. When I found her sweet spot, she said, "Shit, Tim, that's it. Damn it, Tim, that's it." She tried to run but I held her there. I could tell that she was trying to keep from coming. That ass was jumping around like it had springs under it. Then all of a sudden her body tensed up. She let out the loudest scream I ever heard.

I said, "Oh, my God, she's coming and pissing all at the same time." I had never seen that before. I had made her come so hard she pissed on herself.

She was so embarrassed. She said, "This has never happened before." After we got a towel and covered the spot, we continued. It got so rough the bed collapsed. The slats had given way. She said, "I never had this problem until you came along."

I said, "That's OK. You aren't getting away that easy." We fixed the bed and continued—this time doggy style. We were a little gentler this time.

Then she turned and said, "Ooooooooh, Mr. Sawyer." I felt like someone had rammed a steel beam in my penis. The tone of her voice and the look of ecstasy in her eyes made me so excited, I got that much harder instantly. Then we got off together for the last time.

The next morning we got up to go to work. She ironed my shirt and fixed me breakfast. I went to work feeling like a king. She gave me a key when I was going out the door along with a kiss.

When I got to work my brother Mike called. He asked where I had been. Because he hadn't heard from me or seen me in a while, I told him what was going on. I told him I was staying with Gina and how I was being treated. He said, "Enjoy it while it lasts. You know that shit ain't going to last forever."

I said, "I know, but damn, it's good to be the king."

As time went on, the sex was cool but I noticed changes in me. My spirit was starting to trouble me. I would listen to the gospel station every morning. It shortly became the only thing I wanted to listen to. Gina started complaining. She really wasn't into gospel. She asked me how I could sin all night and praise God in the morning. That kind of baffled me. Then out of my mouth came, "This ain't going to last long."

On my way to work this day, I was listening to my favorite station. A song came on that said, "Trouble don't last always." This hit me like a ton of bricks. I got filled with joy instantly.

A few weeks went by and God opened up a way for me to get my own house. This was such a blessing. I knew Gina and I weren't spiritually compatible. I knew I was far from perfect. I also knew I had to go a different direction if I was ever going to make it.

It was a Wednesday. I remembered a friend that I grew up with had a church in Springfield. I went to Bible study that night. The service was good. He talked about how he had been caught up in addiction and God delivered him. That really gave me hope. I always

prayed for deliverance, but I seemed to keep coming back to drugs/
alcohol.

After church I waited around to talk to him. I approached him. He recognized me right away. We embraced and shook hands. He said, "What's happening, Sawyer?" I told him I had moved to Springfield. I told him I really needed to talk to him. He said he didn't have time; he was getting ready to go on vacation. This really pissed me off. Here he is a minister—not only that, but one I grew up with. He didn't even have ten minutes for me. That just about did me in. That night I went out on the block and bought me some dope. I thought, *Here I go again.*

A few days went by. Things were not going bad at all. Man, Gina was buying me all kinds of stuff. She gave me stuff for my house and everything. She asked me when she was going to get a key. I said, "You're not, and here is your key." I felt kind of strange doing this, but I know it was the right thing to do. I had recognized things in her that I did not like. I wasn't going to settle. That's what I did with Donna and look where it got me. I still didn't stop the relationship, because there were some other attributes, if you know what I mean. If it wasn't for her being so evil and judgmental and thinking she was right about everything, we would probably still be together to this day. Even then, I was looking for someone I could be faithful to and really build something with.

The Lord was really working on me. Here I was—the biggest whore, partier, and part-time drug dealer—and I seriously wanted to change. I mean, I really felt it in my heart. I would pray and ask God to lead me. He was, although I couldn't see it. You probably can't either, but you will later.

Sunday came and someone told me about a church called the Greater Grace Temple. I got up and got dressed and went to church. As soon as I hit the door, a feeling came over me. It was one that I hadn't felt before. It really made me feel good. I got in the sanctuary. The praise and worship team was slammin'. I said, "OK, I'm with it." Then it happened. The pastor came out. He had on a blue sweater and tan pants. He was a fair-skinned brother. Then I realized I had been here in a dream that I had when I was in Indianapolis. It was so strong. All of a sudden I knew where I was supposed to be.

Christmas came and went. It was now January 2003. I went and got my two youngest children, Nikki and Tony, and brought them to live with me. Donna and Tim came up also. She said she wanted to see where her children were going to be living. Tim wanted to stay with his mom. He had some little girl he was sniffing around and at that time it was stronger than his desire to be with his dad.

I showed them around the house. Instantly, Nikki and Tony said, "Where is my room?" I could see the jealousy on Donna's face. She couldn't believe I was doing this all by myself. She could see I really didn't need her. She was merely in my life because I wanted her there. I was beginning to see that everything I wanted was not good for me.

I got my children registered in school. Nikki (my chocolate) settled in right away and Tony—well, let's just say Tony was being Tony. I would get up in the morning and fix their breakfast and take them to school. I really enjoyed that. Nikki had to be there first. I would take her and come back and get Tony. Nikki would always give me a kiss when she got out of the car and say, "I love you, Dad."

When I dropped Tony off, we would dap and he might say, "I love you," if he didn't have an attitude.

Tony was my demon child. He was always in trouble at school. It was always someone else's fault. That boy could really lie. I wonder where he got that from—probably his mom. Anyway, he had a real sweet heart but he could flip on a dime. I think he had just been spoiled too much because of him getting sick at a young age. For the longest time I thought his learning disability came from Donna smoking dope while she was pregnant. But later I found out that it was something in the man that would have as big a factor. So I can't really blame her. I am just as much to blame. I'm so glad he turned out as good as he did. In fact, he's getting better all the time, thank God. Some time went by. Gina met my children. Nikki was stand-offish, but I guess that's a girl thing. After all, she was fresh from leaving her mom and she didn't want anything coming between her and her dad. Tony was cool because, as usual, all women thought he was so cute and spoiled him. That was part of his problem. Time went on. Things were going pretty good. I was making good money. All we had in the house right then was bedroom furniture, dining room furniture, and a TV, but we were content for the time being.

Spring came. Business picked up at the lot. I went and bought some furniture and a Caddy. Things were really getting good, mainly because I was trying to change my ways. I was even tithing now— well, sometimes. At least I was making an effort. I had cut back on my drug use also. I still couldn't completely stop.

About March or April Donna called. I was telling her how we should stay apart because things were starting to get better. Then she put this guilt trip on me. She said every time I moved away and wanted to come back, she took me in. I told her it was because she needed me so she could live the lifestyle she liked to live with my money. She got upset and told me if she lost her apartment I had to take her in. I should have known then she was setting me up. She stopped paying her rent so they would put her out. I know also she was still smoking, but then so was I. The difference was that I was making almost seventy thousand dollars a year and she was only making about twenty-five.

It's funny how when things start attacking your spirit, all the money, the women, the clothes, and the cars really don't matter. What I wanted most was to stop using drugs and to have a woman I could love and be faithful to.

I started noticing little changes in myself—for instance, the women at Greater Grace were looking real good, but I couldn't say anything to them. Even though my flesh wanted me to, my spirit wouldn't let me. The player in me was starting to die. I knew I was getting better. It felt real strange though. Whenever the thought to say something slick came to mind, I found myself saying to myself, *Shut up, Tim.* There was one special lady there that I was always attracted to, but I knew it wasn't right.

As I could see God working in my life, it baffled me that I could not leave drugs/alcohol alone. But I was grateful that my sexual addiction was starting to subside. Then I started to realize that the street mentality kept me sick—wanting instant gratification. I realized the player had to die for the man to live.

June 2003 came. School was out. Sure enough, Donna had to move out of her apartment. I went and got her stuff and moved her in. My brother was upset. He told me, "Every time you get out on your own, things start going good. Then Donna and you get back together. The bottom falls out." He said, "I'll give you a year and you are going to lose everything." Well, it took two. I can't blame everything on her. I was too weak to resist her. It seems awfully strange. I knew I was not perfect. I also knew that when we got together it was worse. And it did get worse. Instantly we started getting high. It was the same old routine: getting high and having sex. It seemed that was all we had together and I was sick of it.

One day I went over to my friend's house as I often did. We would sit over there and drink. Occasionally, his ex-sister-in-law would come by and we would sit and talk stuff. Donna had asked me earlier if she could have the car to go to Dayton. I told her no, I was going over to Poncho's. My spirit told me she was up to something. When I got home she was dressed like she was going out. I guess I got home too early. She told me a girlfriend from work was coming to get her. I said OK. Then she said she was going to meet her at the Speedway station up the street. I told her I would go with her so she wouldn't have to bring the car back. We got up there. She said she wasn't there. We went back to the house. She grabbed the cordless phone and went upstairs. I could tell she was agitated by the way she was acting. She was trying to use the phone to call her friend. I went upstairs after her and acted like I was looking for something. She went back downstairs and I followed her. Something told me to let her use the phone. So I lingered inside and then came out and sat on the porch. She dialed some numbers and acted like she was talking. Then she hung up. Then she said her friend was coming to the house. I told her to let me use the phone. I hit redial and only three numbers were dialed. I didn't say anything. She said her friend was going to be in a white car. I told her, "When she gets here, tell her to come in and see your house."

She quickly said, "We don't have time for all that." About that time a white car pulled up at the corner. She waved them down. The car went past the house, turned around, and pulled up on the side. As she went down, I said I was going to say hi to her friend. We got to the car. There were two men in it. Then she said, "Oh, it's the wrong car." We went back up on the porch. I guess I was so stunned I was numb.

Then the phone rang. I could hear a man's voice saying, "I don't want any trouble."

She said, "I don't either." I didn't say much about it then, but as I write about it now, I'm having a few feelings. I'm mostly glad I'm not with her. In fact, I am in another treatment center writing this book. This is another attempt to break away.

Time has passed since that incident and things got progressively worse—getting high and drinking. I guess, looking back, I was trying to stuff my feelings. I was always taught that players didn't feel and now I see why. When that incident happened with the guys coming to pick her up, a normal person would have went off. Instead, I just stayed away from her for a while and slept on the couch. As time went on, I guess Donna could see that I was upset even though I tried not to let it show. This was really hard—acting as if nothing had happened. I didn't want to run around chasing women even though I didn't want to be with her. When we had sex I felt like I was masturbating inside her. I mean, there was just nothing there. I didn't have the urge to please her anymore. We went on much the same way for a while.

In May of 2004 I got preapproved for a house loan. I told the lady that I was renting from and she said I could buy that house. When I told her, she went up on the price from $74.9 thousand to $82.9 thousand. I knew how much work the house needed, so I offered her $69.9 thousand. She told me that she guessed I wouldn't be buying it. I told her I would be moving in a month. I told her she could keep my security deposit for the last month's rent. She didn't like that much and she had me evicted.

We put all our stuff in storage and moved into my mom's house in Dayton. Mind you, my children were still in school and I still had to go to work in Springfield. Needless to say, this was very stressful. We had been looking and looking for a house, but we never could quite get together on a deal. All these houses were in the sixty- to seventy-thousand-dollar range. I thought that would be my comfort zone. I wanted to stay around the six-hundred- to seven-hundred-dollar range per month.

One day I was sitting in my mom's TV room. Something spoke to me in my spirit and said, *Tim, you are not looking deep enough.* So I talked to my realtor and asked her what a one-hundred-thousand-dollar house would cost per month. She said, "About eight hundred dollars per month."

I said, "OK, let's try that."

I looked at a couple of houses. When we walked into this one house on East Cassilly Street, my spirit said, *This is your house.*

I asked, "How much is this one?" She said, "One hundred ten thousand."

I said, "OK, let's do it." This house fell right in my lap. I found out I would need $6,500. I didn't have it. I got discouraged and you know what I did? Smoked some more dope.

When I got back to my mom's, my mortgage broker called. He asked where I was, because we were supposed to be in Springfield signing papers for the house. I explained that I didn't have the down payment so I figured the deal was dead. He told me to just come and sign the papers and we would work that out later.

I was riding up Blairwood and Donna was coming down the street. We stopped and she asked me where I had been. I told her I had been over at the dope house. She said, "I figured that." I told her the mortgage broker called. I followed her to park her car and we rode to Springfield.

When we got there, my mortgage broker said he had the down payment worked out. He said, "Just go ahead and do the paperwork and we will take care of the money tomorrow." It seemed the down payment dropped right in my lap also. God was really working in my life in spite of my indiscretions. I was really trying to be righteous. I had pretty much stopped chasing women. I just couldn't stop getting high.

This ended up being one of the most miserable times in my life. You would think that buying a new house, and making plenty of money on my job, things would appear to be on the upswing. *Wrong.* Actually, the plane was just leaving the runway, starting to climb, and when it reached cruising altitude all hell broke loose.

Our addiction got worse. We would stay up all night using sometimes and still go to work. How I made it only God knows. I understand that it was only his grace and mercy that were keeping me.

I was fighting the addiction with everything I had. I was going to church twice a week. I was paying my tithes whenever I could. I knew that God would be the only thing that could save me. I would talk to my pastor about what was going on and he would tell me, "Tim, just hold on. It's only a test that you are going through." He said, "The closer you try to get to the Lord, the more Satan is going to fight you." I couldn't understand why I was still going through this.

One of the other ministers in the church told me, "Sometimes God will deliver some people right away. Others he will leave in the fire a little while longer—to allow them to suffer a little longer, so he can have a witness." This didn't make me feel much better, but I wasn't going to give up. Even when he told me it was probably going to get worse, I was still determined to hold to God's unchanging hand. And get worse it did.

First, we were getting high so much that when school came around I didn't have money to buy school clothes. Then in October, Nikki, my seventeen-year-old, had a baby. Christmas came and I didn't have any money for Christmas. Man, this plane was coming down fast.

In January, my job made me take a drug test and it came back positive. Through all of this I was still praying and holding on. I still couldn't stop.

In May, the plane crashed. It didn't stop tumbling right away. It rolled a little while longer. I lost my job. I had bought another car before I lost my job. Now that was in jeopardy with my house also, because by now I was a couple months behind on my house payments, to the tune of eleven hundred dollars per month. But did I stop smoking dope? *Noooo!!*

By now the prayer had changed from "God help me," to "Just let me die if I have to live like this." I couldn't seem to get a job anywhere. When I did, I wasn't making anything near the money I was making at my other job. There was just no traffic. Plus my mind was so ate up. I was taking cars off the lot and going by known drug spots in broad daylight. And I had one of my dealers that was selling bottles of liquor. I would take the dealership car and go pick it up and sell it at the dealership. Soon I got fired from that job also.

By June I went to work in Columbus, which was sixty miles one-way. I did pretty good my first month, but it still wasn't enough to get out of the hole. I had hoped, though.

Now I was trying to refinance my house. This was July 2005. In the midst of doing that, I was getting in deeper with my dope dealer. I kept promising him that as soon as I got the money from the house, I would pay him. I had always paid him before. He didn't have any reason not to trust me.

I sold one of my cars. I said I was doing it to pay bills. Donna and I used most of it getting high. She started stealing dope from me and wanting to clean the can, and she would get so pissed at me if I wouldn't let her do it. I thought if the drugs meant that much to her what else was she doing to get it. By being in the streets I had seen what girls would do to get high. By now she didn't want to have sex with me. And I really didn't want her either. I didn't trust her anymore.

Now my house was in foreclosure. This was September 2005. I wrecked my Bonneville—the car that I bought before I lost my job. I didn't have any insurance. Now I just wanted to kill myself. I was standing out on Limestone Street waiting for a truck to come by so I could walk out in front of it. If it hadn't have been for a couple of church members seeing the accident and standing there talking to me, I would have walked out in front of the first truck I saw. I know now that God was working in my life. Did I stop using? No!

By October I had started loaning my car out. This is something I used to talk about people for doing. This was the only car I had that was worth a damn. It was Donna's only way of getting to work. Donna was OK with it. She used to ask me if I knew anyone I could let use the car. That's when I figured that as long as she could blame it on me, she didn't care what we did.

One night I loaned the car out to a guy named T. T didn't get back to where he left me until 6:30a.m. Donna had to be at work at 5:00a.m. I had already called her and told her to call in. I went off on T. I was getting ready to do him right there. He got scared. I guess he could see death in my eyes. At that point he said, "Hold on, man. Tim, hold on. I got you." We were sitting in the car in front of his house. At this time he gave me some dope and money for gas and I left.

I got home at about five minutes to seven. I asked Donna if Tony had left for school. She said yes, so I closed my bedroom door and locked it. When I sat down on the bed, my back door opened and closed. I said, "I thought Tony was gone."

She said, "He is." Now normally when we would hear a noise in the house, she would be the first to say, "Go check it out." This time she wasn't concerned. She obviously knew who was in there. After all, if she was bold enough to have a guy come to the house to pick her up, why wouldn't she have someone in the house?

This really put a strain on our relationship. I didn't want to touch her. I didn't want her to touch me. All we did for the next month was get high. This was November. I had a moment of clarity. I called my nephew's dad and told him I wanted to check myself into treatment. He said when I got ready, he'd got me. The plane stopped tumbling. The player was dead.

The player had to die so that the man could live. I had finally been whipped to the point of surrender. God had to let me get just enough pain, until I knew without a doubt that it was him and only him that could save me.

This happened after months of embarrassment, going to food pantries, and asking the church for money for groceries and to pay bills. To think that I was a man on track to make over one hundred thousand dollars in 2005. The use of drugs brought me to my knees. I see how that street player mentality took me right back to where I was in 1989.

I used to think that this time wasn't so bad, but in actuality it was worse. In 1989 I really didn't have anything to lose. This time, I lost a $100,000-a-year job, three cars, and a $110,000 home in one year. God allowed me to get to this point for me to see the error of my ways and to make a new start.

In 1989, I promised him that if he saved me from that life, I would always trust in him and do the right thing. The first thing I did as soon as I got on my feet was start chasing women and selling weed. I still hadn't let go of that street player mentality. The player had to die. You can't serve two masters. See, I couldn't see at that time that everything I had learned to do so early in life was all wrong. I was taught real early in life how to lie, cheat, and manipulate women. I was also taught that it was OK to be married and have other women.

I had watched my dad, his friends, my uncles, and my cousins for as long as I could remember do that very thing. So it's no wonder how I had that same conception. After so long, I couldn't blame my behavior on them. I started to feel that what I was doing was wrong.

I watched Antonio (my son) as he was in preschool—how he would go to school and curse his teachers out. They thought he had learned it from me. I was so confused. Out of all the wrong that I done, my children never saw me do any of it. I knew I didn't talk like that around him. One day I was in my bedroom. He and his older sister were in her room dancing and listening to rap music. Then the light came on. They had been doing this for years and that's where he learned that language. I whipped his butt for the longest time, trying to get that spirit out of him.

That's the same thing God did to me. He had to allow me to get enough pain—that is, whipping—in order to get me to realize that I had to change my ways. This meant I had to not just stop getting high. The answer was spiritual and until I started trying to act spiritually, I couldn't stop getting high.

Now I'm sitting in the Prospect House, one of the premiere treatment facilities in the country, and as much as I thought I knew about God, I realize that I didn't know as much as I thought.

For instance, I had to turn my will and my whole life over to the care of God and get out of the way. I have to pray every night and day for him to lead me and guide me. I've learned that having all the women, money, cars, clothes, and houses doesn't mean anything if I don't have myself and God.

Since I have been here at the PH, I have decided to totally commit my ways to the Lord, to live clean and sober the rest of my days, and to wait on the Lord to send me a woman that I can share all my love with and make her my wife and give her pleasures she's never known.

The player is truly dead!!!

Breinigsville, PA USA
17 September 2009

224263BV00002B/4/P